# GREAT BATTLES OF THE WAFFEN-SS

# GREAT BATTLES OF THE WAFFEN-SS

**General Editor: Peter Darman**

Grange
BOOKS

This edition published in 2004 by Grange Books

Grange Books plc

The Grange

1–6 Kingsnorth Estate

Hoo

Near Rochester

Kent ME3 9ND

www.grangebooks.co.uk

ISBN 1-84013-682-0

Printed in China

Editorial and design:

The Brown Reference Group plc

8 Chapel Place

Rivington Street

London

EC2A 3DQ

UK

www.brownreference.com

# CONTENTS

# Key to maps

## Military units – types

⊠  infantry

◣  armoured

▱  motorized infantry/
   panzergrenadier

☂  parachute/airborne

## Military units – size

XXXXX
☐  army group/front

XXXX
☐  army

XXX
☐  corps

XX
☐  division

III
☐  regiment

## Military unit colours

▦  Soviet

▦  German

▦  British and
   Commonwealth

▦  US

## Military movements (in national colours)

➡  attack

⦙⦙⦙▶  retreat

## General military symbols (in national colours)

——  frontline

⋀⋁  defensive line

⬭  pocket

## Geographical symbols

—•—  railway line

——  river

●  urban area

⬠  urban area

–··–··–  country boundary

————  road

🌳  trees

〰  marsh

⫽  bridge

# WAFFEN-SS DIVISIONAL INSIGNIA

1st SS Panzer
Division
*Leibstandarte*

2nd SS Panzer
Division
*Das Reich*

*Das Reich*
Kursk marking

3rd SS Panzer
Division
*Totenkopf*

5th SS Panzer
Division
*Wiking*

9th SS Panzer
Division
*Hohenstaufen*

10th SS Panzer
Division
*Frundsberg*

12th SS Panzer
Division
*Hitlerjugend*

# CHAPTER 1

# KHARKOV

## I SS Panzer Corps wins its spurs and saves Army Group South.

On 14 March 1943, German radio interrupted its normal broadcasts with a fanfare from the Horst Wessel song (a Nazi anthem commemorating the death of a stormtrooper during a street battle in the 1920s), and announced that Waffen-SS troops had recaptured the Ukrainian city of Kharkov. The five-day battle to win control of the Soviet Union's fourth-largest city was the culmination of a two-month campaign by the Wehrmacht's Army Group South to turn back the advancing Russians after the destruction of the German Sixth Army at Stalingrad. German radio was right to give the success such prominence. In January, Stalin's armies had been running rampant in the Ukraine, with the Wehrmacht falling back in disarray after the massive defeat suffered by the German Army. Over 150,000 Germans died on the banks of the Volga and a further 91,000, including their commander, Field Marshal Friedrich Paulus, surrendered despite being ordered to fight to the last man by their Führer, Adolf Hitler. While finishing off the remnants of Paulus' battered army, the Russians extended their offensive to the Ukraine, smashing weak German, Hungarian and Italian armies in their path. By early February 1943, Soviet tanks were pushing towards the River Dnieper. Kharkov was threatened, and Russian spearheads were moving south to cut off German troops retreating from the Caucasus through Rostov.

Stalin's generals, however, underestimated the resilience of the Wehrmacht. Army Group South's commander, Field Marshal Erich von Manstein, concentrated his still-powerful panzer divisions and hit the Russians with a stunning counter-punch, just as they reached the limit of their supply lines. The Soviets found themselves out-

■ *Left:* Waffen-SS men steel themselves for the Battle for Kharkov. Russia's winter tested the strength and endurance of Hitler's élite panzer force to the limit.

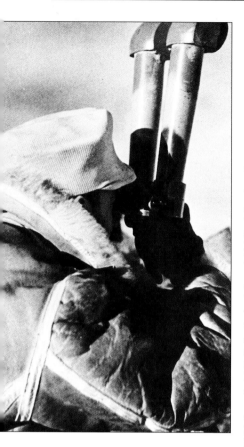

ported by the 88th and 168th Infantry Divisions, held the Belgorod area. Two divisions of the SS Panzer Corps, which had just arrived from France, were deployed along the Donets blocking the direct route to Kharkov.

Under SS-Obergruppenführer Paul Hausser, I SS Panzer Corps was superbly equipped with new tanks, armoured half-track personnel carriers, self-propelled artillery and Nebelwerfer multi-barrel rocket launchers. Holding the Donets line were the *Leibstandarte* and *Das Reich* Divisions. The 1st SS Panzer Regiment of the *Leibstandarte* was the strongest tank unit in the corps, with 52 Panzer IVs, 10 Panzer IIIs and nine Tiger Is. *Das Reich*'s 2nd SS Panzer Regiment had 81 Panzer IIIs and only 21 Panzer IVs, backed up by 10 Tiger Is.

## A long journey

The journey from France took almost two weeks, and many of the 200 trains carrying the division were re-routed to avoid Royal Air Force (RAF) bombing and Soviet partisan attacks. These disruptions meant that the divisions arrived at the railhead in Kharkov in dribs and drabs. The first elements to arrive were from the *Leibstandarte*'s 1st Panzergrenadier Regiment, which threw an improvised defensive ring around Kharkov along the frozen banks of the River Donets. Next off the trains on 29 January were the armoured cars and motorcycles of the *Leibstandarte*'s reconnaissance battalion, and they were dispatched to set up a covering screen 80km (50 miles) to the east, to give early warning of any approaching Russians. At the same time the *Deutschland* Panzergrenadier Regiment, of the *Das Reich* Division, was also sent to extend the screen northwards.

As the Waffen-SS troops fanned out across the winter wasteland, they had a series of vicious encounters with the advance guard of the Soviet XVIII Guards Corps. Intermingled with the Russian troops were retreating columns of the hard-pressed German 298th and 320th Infantry Divisions, who had marched across the steppe to seek safety in the west. The German infantry columns were shepherded back towards Kharkov. In a couple of cases,

■ *Left:* Unlike during the Battle for Moscow in 1941, Waffen-SS troops fighting in the Kharkov campaign were well equipped with winter clothing and equipment.

flanked and outgunned. They still had a lot to learn about armoured warfare.

Soviet forces began the final phase of their offensive on 14 January with a massive attack on the overstretched German, Hungarian and Italian armies dug-in along the River Don. Lieutenant-General F.I. Golikov's Voronezh Front and Lieutenant-General N.F. Vatutin's Southwest Front rolled over the defenders with ease and, within two weeks, had pushed 160km (100 miles) westwards. They were now poised to cross the River Donets, which barred the way to Kharkov and the strategically crucial River Dnieper crossings.

To counter this advance, the Germans rushed reinforcements from all over Europe in a desperate bid to rebuild the Eastern Front. North of Kharkov, the army's élite *Grossdeutschland* Motorized Division, sup-

the Waffen-SS reconnaissance troops mounted raids to rescue recently captured infantrymen, racing into Soviet positions on their motorcycles and raking them with machine-gun fire.

The reconnaissance screen fell back deliberately towards Kharkov, and by 4 February 1943 I SS Panzer Corps was almost fully deployed in its main defensive position along the Donets. South of Kharkov there was a void of 160km (100 miles) between the Waffen-SS corps and the left flank of the First Panzer Army. Manstein was moving up units of the Fourth Panzer Army to fill the gap, but they would take time to arrive, leaving Kharkov very exposed to encirclement by Golikov's tanks in the interim.

Hausser's Waffen-SS troops held their front along the Donets with grim determination against furious attacks by the Soviet XII and XV Tank Corps (a Soviet tank corps was equivalent in tank strength to a German panzer division) from Lieutenant-General

*The Waffen-SS divisions inflicted heavy casualties against Soviet human-wave attacks*

P.S. Rybalko's Third Tank Army until 10 February (each tank army had two tank corps, a separate tank brigade and support units). This brave stand only played into the Soviets' hands. Russian troops were pushing around the flanks of Hausser's corps and there was a real prospect of Stalingrad being repeated, albeit on a much smaller scale. Major-General K.S. Moskalenko's Fortieth Army, with IV Tank Corps in the lead, turfed the *Grossdeutschland* Division out of Belgorod and sent it heading south to Kharkov.

In their positions east of the city, the Waffen-SS divisions inflicted heavy casualties against Soviet human-wave attacks. Hausser, now dubbed "Papa" by his men, took great delight in visiting the frontline to watch the action. He was reportedly particularly impressed by the performance of the new MG 42 belt-fed machine gun, which was used in action by the Waffen-SS for the first time by the *Leibstandarte*'s 1st Panzergrenadier Regiment on 4 February.

■ *Above:* Heavy MG 34 machine-gun detachments inflicted massive casualties on Russian human-wave infantry attacks across the barren steppe outside Kharkov.

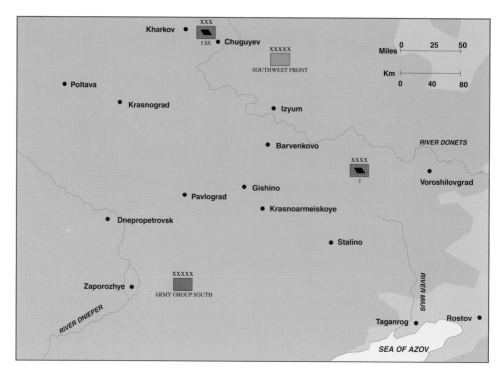

■ **Above:** Strategic situation in the Kharkov area, January 1943.

Hundreds of dead Russians were later found piled in front of the Waffen-SS position.

This was a see-saw battle, with daily Soviet probing attacks and regular German counterattacks. The brunt of these assaults were borne by the Waffen-SS panzer-grenadiers, backed up by small assault gun detachments. Paul Hausser was keeping his panzer regiments well behind the frontline, ready to deal with any major enemy penetration of his front.

To the south of the Waffen-SS, Vatutin took advantage of the lack of opposition in front of him to push his troops tirelessly forward. The Sixth Army, with two tank corps, two infantry corps and a cavalry corps raced for the Dnieper crossing at Dnepropetrovsk, while Lieutenant-General M.M. Popov's Front Mobile Group of four tank corps pushed south, aiming for Krasnoarmeiskoye and the Sea of Azov.

> *A strong covering force was to remain around Kharkov under command of Das Reich*

Overestimating the capabilities of his prized Waffen-SS troops, Hitler ordered them to attack southeastwards to close the gap with the First Panzer Army. Two groups were formed for the operation. A strong covering force was to remain around Kharkov under command of *Das Reich*, which also included the *Leibstandarte*'s 2nd Panzergrenadier Regiment and elements of the division's Tiger tank company, artillery and flak regiments. Hausser's corps headquarters and the *Grossdeutschland* Division also remained in the city, along with the 298th Infantry Division.

The covering force fought an increasingly desperate defensive battle, and the frontline had to be pulled back to free troops for the coming operation to the south of the city. By 12 February, the Soviet VI Guards Cavalry Corps had punched a hole in the

■ *Left:* Waffen-SS panzergrenadiers had to fight a series of brutal battles to hold key villages dominating the approaches to Kharkov.

line separating the *Leibstandarte* from the 320th Infantry Division. Surrounded and burdened with thousands of wounded men, the army division needed help fast. A kampfgruppe was formed under SS-Sturmbannführer Joachim Peiper, then commander of the 2nd Panzergrenadier Regiment's armoured personnel carrier battalion, to rescue the division. He was given a column of ambulances and a detachment of StuG III assault guns for the mission. The kampfgruppe punched through the Russian front after destroying several tanks, and pushed 48km (30 miles) behind enemy lines to find the beleaguered infantry division. After loading up the ambulances,

Peiper's men headed back to German lines, but a Soviet ski battalion had moved into place to block their path and destroy the main bridge over the River Udy, which the Waffen-SS column had to cross to return to Kharkov. The Waffen-SS kampfgruppe attacked and cleared out the Russians in house-to-house fighting, before repairing the bridge for the ambulances.

However, the improvised structure could not take the heavy Waffen-SS assault guns and armoured halftracks, so Peiper ordered his men back behind Russian lines to find a more suitable crossing. They returned to the *Leibstandarte*'s lines after suffering only a handful of casualties and rescuing the 320th

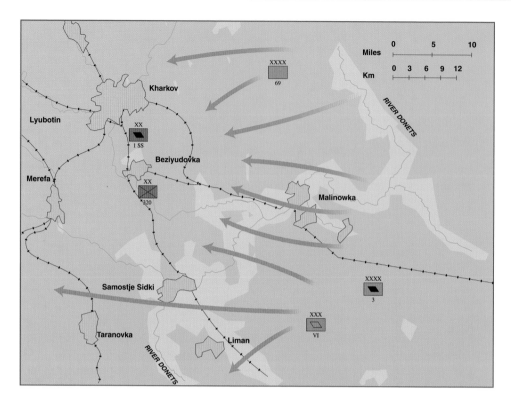

Infantry Division, which was soon able to return to frontline duty after being fed and housed by the Waffen-SS supply units. This was only a temporary respite for Hausser, though. To the north of Kharkov, the *Grossdeutschland* Division was being pushed back into the northern outskirts of the city. No forces could be spared to counter this dangerous pincer because of Hitler's insistence that I SS Panzer Corps' attack group continue with its southward push from Merefa. This would involve the commitment of the *Leibstandarte*'s powerful panzer regiment for the first time.

The large attack group, under the *Leibstandarte*'s commander, SS-Obergruppenführer Josef "Sepp" Dietrich, was ordered to lead the attack forward on 11 February. Pushing directly southwards into the flank of the Soviet VI Guards Cavalry Corps was the *Leibstandarte*'s 1st Panzergrenadier Regiment with its lorry-borne infantry, and the 2nd Battalion of the

division's panzer regiment. *Das Reich*'s *Der Führer* Panzergrenadier Regiment reinforced this effort, while SS-Obersturmbannführer Kurt "Panzer" Meyer led the *Leibstandarte*'s reconnaissance battalion deployed on the right to seal the Russian incursion with a large flanking move. He was given a full panzer battalion to support this daring move.

Heavy snow drifts slowed the advance and made it impossible for the Waffen-SS panzers to take the lead in the attack for the first few hours. Stuka dive-bombers strafed Russian columns, and the Waffen-SS units made good progress, clearing the enemy from village after village. By early evening Meyer and his men had all but completed their encircling move, while the main attack columns surprised and destroyed a number of Russian formations. On 12 February, Meyer's advance continued under the cover of a massive snowstorm. Russian and German tank columns became intermingled in the poor visibility conditions, but the

■ *Above:* Situation east and south of Kharkov, 10–13 February 1943.

Waffen-SS column pressed on regardless. The following day, Meyer's kampfgruppe found itself cut off in Bereka, which blocked the Soviet line of retreat from the pocket created by the Waffen-SS operation. During the night, six tanks of the *Leibstandarte*'s Panzer Regiment, under Max Wünsche, broke through the Soviet ring to reinforce Meyer, and he then used the tanks to sweep the neighbourhood of Soviet infantry. For the next two days the attack group tightened the grip on the trapped Russian cavalry

■ *Above:* The stalwart T-34/76 tank was the mainstay of the Russian tank forces pressing forward against the Waffen-SS defenders inside Kharkov.

■ *Left:* A squad of tank-riding Soviet infantry mount T-34/76s for a breakthrough operation against German defences, February 1943.

■ *Right:* Russian tank commanders receive their orders for a coming attack. By 1943, Soviet staff officers were expert at undertaking complex mobile operations.

corps, and swept village after village for stragglers. *Leibstandarte* panzers led these attacks, neutralizing isolated Russian tanks so the panzergrenadiers could move forward in their armoured halftracks. By the time the Waffen-SS had finished its work, the 7000 Soviet soldiers of VI Guards Cavalry Corps had been scattered, 10 of its 16 tanks destroyed, 3000 troops wounded and a further 400 captured. Other Russian troops were moving forward to help their comrades, however, and soon the Waffen-SS attack group found itself under attack on three fronts. It was now time for the attack group to fall back.

The main Soviet force dodged Hausser's punch, slipping in behind the advancing Waffen-SS men to try to cut them off from Kharkov and split up the already fragmented German front even more. These were desperate days for the Waffen-SS panzer troops. With temperatures dropping to minus 40 degrees centigrade, it was vital to hold towns or villages to provide vital shelter from the elements. Retreat into the freezing night

*Repeated orders from Hitler to hold the city to the last man and bullet were treated with contempt*

spelt disaster, so the Waffen-SS grenadiers were literally fighting for their own survival.

In these see-saw battles the superior equipment, training and determination of the Waffen-SS tank crews usually meant they came out on top, but their panzer kampfgruppen could not be everywhere, and by 14 February Kharkov was virtually surrounded. To compound the problem, an uprising had broken out in the city and Hausser feared that his corps headquarters units, *Das Reich* and *Grossdeutschland* would share the same fate as Paulus at Stalingrad. He wanted to order an evacuation through a narrow corridor to the southwest. Repeated orders from Hitler to hold the city to the last man and bullet were treated with the contempt they deserved. Confusion reigned in the German High Command in the Ukraine, with no one wanting to be seen to disobey the Führer's direct orders. In the end, though, Hausser issued the orders to pull out on 15 February. By the time Hitler found out and had issued countermanding orders, the *Das Reich*

Division was on its way to safety and there was no going back. The *Das Reich* and *Leibstandarte* panzergrenadiers set up an improvised defence line to the south of Kharkov, but Soviet tanks were close on their heels, inflicting a steady stream of casualties before the Waffen-SS units could break clear.

With I SS Panzer Corps safely out of Kharkov, Manstein was able to complete the reorganization of his panzer divisions for their counterstroke. An unannounced visit by Hitler, furious at the loss of Kharkov, to Manstein's headquarters at Zaporozhe on 17 February interrupted the field marshal's preparations. Hitler had intended to dismiss Manstein for the loss of the city and order an immediate northwards attack by I SS Panzer Corps to retake Kharkov. Fortunately for the field marshal, the sound of Russian artillery near his command post brought the Führer to his senses and he left in a hurry, to allow Manstein to get on with sorting out the Soviets. Manstein was also helped by the fact that the Waffen-SS *Totenkopf* Division got stuck in mud after a sudden thaw during the day, making it unavailable for Hitler's proposed attack.

Manstein's plan called for two Waffen-SS divisions to strike southwest from Krasnograd into the western flank of the Soviet Sixth Army, while the Fourth Panzer Army drove northwards to push the remaining elements of the western Soviet attack force onto the guns of the Waffen-SS panzers. Farther east, the First Panzer Army would take the offensive against Popov's Front Mobile Group and complete the destruction of the Soviet forces west of the River Donets.

The Russians proved easy meat for the panzers. After two months of continuous fighting, Popov's group was down to 50 worn-out tanks and 13,000 men fit for battle. Lieutenant-General F.M. Khatritonov's Sixth Army was in an equally perilous state, with many of its 150 tanks stranded through lack of fuel. Of most help to Manstein, however, were orders from Vatutin (who was still convinced the Germans were retreating) for the Soviet troops to keep advancing.

As this battle was developing, Hausser set about reorganizing his corps for offensive action. The *Leibstandarte* was to be the anvil of the offensive based around Krasnograd, while *Das Reich* and the newly arrived

■ *Left:* Russian submachine gun-armed infantry keep watch for German defenders as T-34/76s inch forward. Once on top of an enemy position, the infantry would clear out any German bunkers still fighting.

*Totenkopf* Division swung south and then northwards, forcing the Russians back onto the guns of the *Leibstandarte*. The arrival of the *Totenkopf* at Krasnograd on the morning of 19 February, with its 81 Panzer IIIs, 22 Panzer IVs, and nine Tiger Is, completed I SS Panzer Corps' order of battle for perhaps its most famous victory. In the afternoon Manstein ordered the attack to proceed.

A 96km (60-mile) road march brought *Das Reich* and *Totenkopf* to their jump-off positions at Novomoskovsk on 20 February. Pushing westwards, they sliced through the immobilized XXV Tank Corps and IV Guards and XV Guards Rifle Corps near Pavlograd. These units were in bad shape after Luftwaffe antitank aircraft caught the Russian armour by surprise earlier in the morning. XXXXVIII Panzer Corps was

already attacking from the south, so the Waffen-SS attack sliced into the side of the already-stalled Russian columns. *Totenkopf* was assigned the northern axis of the attack, and *Das Reich* pushed farther south and then turned eastwards to Pavlograd, before swinging northwards. The Waffen-SS men raced forward at such a break-neck speed that Soviet and German troops often became intermingled. A panzer kampfgruppe of *Das Reich* spearheading the division's advance seized a key bridge outside Pavlograd on 22 February. Two *Das Reich* Panzer IIIs and a Tiger held the bridge for several hours, destroying three T-34s that tried to take the bridge back.

The two Waffen-SS divisions trapped the Soviet I Guards Tank Corps and two rifle divisions. The Waffen-SS Tigers and Panzer IVs knocked out the Russian tanks and antitank guns with ease at long range with their powerful 88mm and 75mm cannons, before panzergrenadiers closed in to mop-up pockets of isolated Soviet infantry who offered resistance in the snow-bound villages. Elements of Soviets divisions were smashed in the attack, with most of the men just abandoning their tanks and vehicles and fleeing into the surrounding forests. For five days the two Waffen-SS divisions meandered through huge columns of abandoned and destroyed vehicles, machine-gunning small groups of Russian soldiers hiding amid the carnage. The Soviet Sixth Army had ceased to exist.

### The death of Theodor Eicke

The Soviets exacted a heavy price on the *Totenkopf* Division for its victory, however. The division's commander, SS-Obergruppenführer Theodor Eicke, flew forward in his Fieseler Storch light aircraft to visit his spearhead units on 26 February. The infamous SS general ordered his pilot to land near a village that he believed was occupied by *Totenkopf* troops. In fact, the men on the ground were a group of cut-off Russian soldiers, and Eicke's aircraft was ripped apart in mid-air by antiaircraft artillery fire as it approached the ground. The following day Waffen-SS troops cleared the village and recovered the mutilated body of the former concentration camp commander.

■ *Left:* SS-Obergruppenführer Paul "Papa" Hausser formed the SS Panzer Corps in France during 1942 and led it into action at Kharkov.

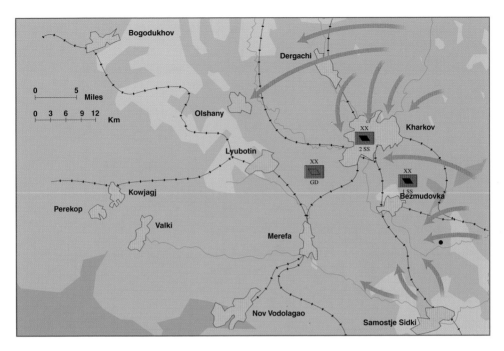

From the north, the *Leibstandarte* Division was conducting an aggressive defence of its line in the snow, aimed at neutralizing the advance elements of the Soviet Third Tank Army. *Leibstandarte* kampfgruppen were launched forward on a daily basis to destroy large Soviet formations spotted by Luftwaffe aerial reconnaissance. The Waffen-SS men infiltrated at night through the thinly held Soviet front to ambush the enemy. Bursting from forests, the kampfgruppen usually took the Russians by surprise, and within minutes their panzers and armoured halftracks would be right in the middle of the enemy positions, spreading mayhem and destruction. Their job complete, the Germans would then pull back to regroup and rearm for the next foray.

On 17 February the *Leibstandarte*'s reconnaissance battalion, reinforced with panzers, wiped out a Soviet infantry regiment in the first big raid. Three days later Peiper's armoured infantry battalion cleared out 750 Russians, three tanks and dozens of antitank guns from a heavily defended village during a night attack.

SS-Obersturmbannführer Kurt "Panzer" Meyer was given command of a kampfgruppe of panzers and reconnaissance troops on 19 February, with the mission of destroying a large enemy forcing advancing westwards. His panzer company destroyed a Russian battalion in the afternoon.

At dawn on 21 February, his column had taken up ambush positions near the town of Jerememkevka. Meyer spotted a long column of Soviet troops moving across the snow-covered steppe, totally unaware of the imminent danger. The attack began with a daredevil charge into the middle of the column by a reconnaissance team in VW Schwimmwagen amphibious jeeps, led by Meyer himself. One vehicle was blown up by a mine, but within minutes the others were among the stunned Russians,

> One vehicle was blown up by a mine, but within minutes they were among the stunned Russians

■ *Above:* Soviet advances to the north and south of Kharkov, 15 February 1943.

raking them with machine-gun fire. Panzer IV tanks then burst out of the woods at the head and tail of the column, cutting off any hope of retreat. Several hundred Russians were slaughtered and a dozen artillery pieces captured. The following night Meyer's force launched another raid on an unsuspecting Russian column, with similar results. The fighting on the northern sector of the division's front was also intense, with the panzer regiment having to be sent to relieve its pioneer battalion, which had been surrounded by a surprise Soviet attack.

On 23 February Meyer's battle group was ordered forward, again ambushing a Soviet divisional headquarters and a whole divisional artillery group. A surprise panzer attack charged into a Russian-held town, and within five hours the *Leibstandarte* men had killed 1000 enemy soldiers and captured 30 heavy artillery pieces.

While the *Leibstandarte*, *Das Reich* and *Totenkopf* Divisions were striking back at the Soviet spearheads south of Kharkov, on the right flank of the German front the *Wiking* Panzergrenadier Division was involved in a series of brutal skirmishes to hold back the enemy advance. A powerful Soviet tank force, led by III and IV Tank Corps and supported by hundreds of ski troops, was pushing south into the breach in the German line, just to the west of the First Panzer Army. Manstein hoped to seal the gap in the front from the west with I SS Panzer Corps, and from the east with the armoured units of the Fourth Panzer Army being brought up from the Caucasus.

By 8 February, the Soviets had taken the key rail junctions at Krasnoarmeiskoye and Gishino, in a surprise push 80km (50 miles) behind the left flank of the First Panzer Army. First on the scene to counter this dangerous incursion was the *Wiking* Division, closely followed by the 7th and 11th Panzer Divisions. These were not fresh and superbly equipped divisions. They had been in action continuously for almost three months, and were down to only 2000 fighting troops each. *Wiking* alone could not

muster more than five battered old Panzer III tanks fit for action. The Waffen-SS men could barely stabilize the front, let alone press forward to clear out the incursion. Only his strong artillery regiment enabled the *Wiking*'s commander, SS-Obergruppenführer Felix Steiner, to contain the Russian tanks.

On 12 February, the *Wiking* Division launched an outflanking attack into the eastern edge of Krasnoarmeiskoye itself and northwards to Gishino, but it broke down in the face of fanatical Soviet resistance. For the next week, the Waffen-SS men and an army infantry division fought vicious street battles to contain the Soviet forces from breaking out of the town. X Soviet Tank Corps arrived to support the advance from Krasnoarmeiskoye, but the Soviet troops in the region were also very

*On the right flank of the German front the* Wiking *Division was involved in a series of brutal skirmishes*

■ *Above:* **Sudden thaws proved a major hurdle to Waffen-SS operations. Prior to Manstein's counteroffensive, the *Totenkopf* Division was stuck for days in mud quagmires.**

weak by this time, with no more than two dozen tanks available to fight the Waffen-SS troops.

The 7th Panzer Division was now thrown into the battle, attacking into the east of the city, while the *Wiking* Division tried to storm in from the west. Luftwaffe Stukas supported the assault, but the Russians held firm. XXXX Panzer Corps now ordered the *Wiking* and the 7th Panzer Divisions to bypass Krasnoarmeiskoye. In a Blitzkrieg-style advance they were to defeat the Soviets in a battle of manoeuvre. The attack opened on 19 February with a sweep north from Krasnoarmeiskoye across the open steppe, trapping several thousand Russians and 12 tanks. A large Soviet force broke out two days later. Now the remaining elements of the Popov Mobile Group turned tail and headed north as fast as possible.

The rearguard of X Tank Corps, with 16 T-34s, tried to halt the *Wiking* Division on 21 February. Again the *Wiking* swept around the Soviet defences and rolled north-wards. This was a no-holes-barred pursuit. The handful of Waffen-SS tanks of the division's only panzer battalion were leading the way, supported by armoured cars and motorcycle troops. Every couple of kilometres, the advance guard would run into the remains of a Soviet vehicle column, either abandoned because of lack of fuel or devastated by Luftwaffe air strikes. The Waffen-SS men did not stop to investigate but pressed on. They did not outnumber the enemy, so victory would only come by moving faster than the Soviets, and keeping enemy commanders confused as to where the Germans would strike next.

The *Wiking*, 7th and 11th Panzer Divisions caught up with the remains of four Soviet infantry divisions and four tank corps at Barvenkovo on 25 February. More than 50 T-34s were dug in to the south of the town, but they had run out of fuel so could not manoeuvre against the rampaging panzers. In a three-day battle, the 11th Panzer Division attacked directly from the

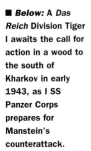

■ *Below:* A *Das Reich* Division Tiger I awaits the call for action in a wood to the south of Kharkov in early 1943, as I SS Panzer Corps prepares for Manstein's counterattack.

south, while the *Wiking* and 7th Panzer Divisions swept around the Russians' flanks. The Soviets, however, kept open a corridor to the Donets at Izyum, and most of their troops managed to escape the pincers – but all their tanks had to be left behind.

By the end of the February the first phase of Manstein's offensive was complete. The Russian thrust to the south had been defeated and the gap in the German front closed by the dramatic intervention of I SS Panzer Corps. The German High Command claimed 615 enemy tanks, 354 artillery pieces, 69 antiaircraft guns destroyed, 23,000 Russians dead and 9000 prisoners, during the first phase of the counterattack. Manstein now turned his attention to the large Soviet armoured force guarding the southern approach to Kharkov. In an ill-considered move to blunt the German drive, Rybalko's Third Tank Army swung south to take on I SS Panzer Corps. In a matter of days his army would be cut to pieces.

> *The Russian thrust to the south had been defeated and the gap in the front closed by I SS Panzer Corps*

The attack got underway on 24 February, with heavy tank attacks against the northern flank of the *Leibstandarte* Division. The frontline panzergrenadier units had to call up panzer support to drive off the Soviet 11th Cavalry Division, for the loss of five tanks and 500 dead. A panzer attack on the following day surprised a Soviet artillery regiment and destroyed more than 50 howitzers. An attack force of 30 German tanks used a valley to advance behind the Russian artillery, and when they broke cover the Soviets fled. Soviet pressure on the *Leibstandarte* Division continued on 26 February, with a heavy tank attack by T-34 medium and KV-1 heavy tanks. A total of 12 vehicles were destroyed by Waffen-SS antitank teams.

The Soviets now pushed their last tank reserves southwards in a bid to drive a wedge between the *Leibstandarte* and its sister divisions, which were moving northwards after they had finished clearing up what was left of the Soviet Sixth Army. Hausser ordered the *Leibstandarte* to pull back on 28 February to entice the Russians to move farther south into a trap. Three days later, I SS Panzer Corps was advancing again. The Luftwaffe caught the Russian tanks in the open and broke up their attack formations.

The *Leibstandarte*'s panzers then moved eastwards, destroying nine tanks and 15 anti-tank guns. A link-up with the *Der Führer* Panzergrenadier Regiment, of the *Das Reich* Division, was made on 3 March. Meyer's reconnaissance battalion achieved another link-up with *Totenkopf* later in the day, to complete the ring around a huge pocket of Soviet troops. For two days infantry elements of I SS Panzer Corps cleared up the pocket, but there were not enough troops and so thousands of Russians escaped. In the *Leibstandarte*'s section of the pocket, prisoners from four Russian infantry divisions and a tank brigade were picked up. VI Guards Cavalry Corps managed to escape the trap, but large parts of IV, XXII and XV Tank Corps were destroyed. A further 61 Soviet tanks, 225 guns, 60 motor vehicles and 9000 dead were left on the icy battlefield.

Rybalko's defeat left Kharkov wide open, and Manstein soon set his panzers rolling north again to capture the prize. He planned to push I SS Panzer Corps forward to bypass Kharkov from the west, and then swing east around the top of the city to the Donets and block the escape route of its defenders, as XXXXVIII Panzer Corps assaulted the city from the south. To complete the victory, the reinforced *Grossdeutschland* Division, which had recently received a new tank detachment of 42 Panzer IVs and nine Tigers, would strike north to Belgorod to block any interference with the attack on Kharkov. It was to be supported by the *Totenkopf*'s reconnaissance battalion during this phase of the operation. Only the imminent arrival of the spring thaw could save Kharkov from the Germans now.

### Closing the trap

Hausser now pulled together his panzer corps into an attack formation, with the *Totenkopf* on the left, *Leibstandarte* in the centre and *Das Reich* on the right. Rocket launchers were positioned to support the attack, and Tiger I tanks moved forward to spearhead the assault operation.

■ *Below:*
**Sturmgeschütz (StuG) III assault guns played a key role in Waffen-SS attacks against Soviet columns south of Kharkov.**

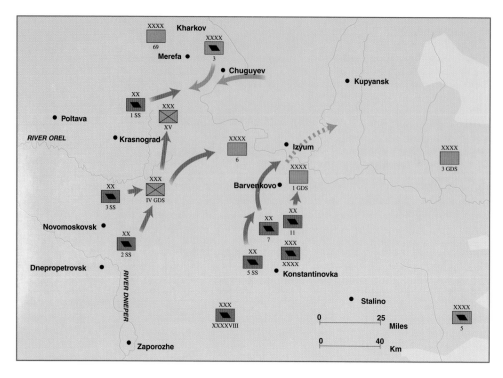

According to plan the first attack went in on 6 March, and four days later the Waffen-SS panzers had reached a line level with Kharkov. To the east, the army panzer divisions were held up for five days by a determined stand by the 25th and 62nd Guards Rifle Divisions.

Heavy air strikes preceded the Waffen-SS advance, with *Das Reich* receiving priority support. The Soviet defences were weak and disorganized, so the German advanced pushed all before it. Again, the *Leibstandarte*'s reconnaissance battalion was teamed with a strong panzer detachment to spearhead the division's advance. This time Meyer had the use of Tiger I tanks for the first time. South of the town of Valki, Meyer's kampfgruppe was confronted by a "pak-front", or network of 56 76.2mm anti-tank guns. With panzergrenadiers sheltering behind the turrets of the tanks, Meyer ordered his panzers to charge forward. Their speed meant Waffen-SS men overran the antitank guns easily, but two dozen T-34 tanks lay in wait ahead, hidden in a village.

The Panzer IVs started to take casualties before a Tiger was called up. The lead Tiger got to within 100m (328ft) of the village when a T-34 opened fire. It hit the Tiger on the turret, but the Soviet 76mm shell barely scratched the German tank's paint. The Tiger blasted the T-34 with its 88mm gun, blowing off the turret and taking half of a nearby house with it. During the next hour the Tigers cleared out a dozen T-34s and the rest fled at high speed. The rest of the kampfgruppe was, meanwhile, clearing out the remaining Soviet infantry and gun crews who had hidden in the village as the tank duel ragged in its streets.

The following day Meyer's men were again confronted by a pak-front on the outskirts of Valki. A tank attack was ordered, but several panzers were lost to enemy fire before they overran the gun pits. German tanks literally crushed the antitank guns under their tracks when the Soviet gunners refused to flee.

*Das Reich*'s *Der Führer* Panzergrenadier Regiment led the division's attack, and it

■ *Above:* Soviet and German attacks south of Kharkov. Position on 24 February 1943.

was soon within striking distance of the western outskirts of Kharkov. The *Totenkopf* Division was not making as good progress out on the left wing because of heavy resistance from VI Guards Cavalry Corps. The *Totenkopf*'s reconnaissance battalion was also fighting with the *Grossdeutschland* Division's left-flank units and was unable to help out, after getting bogged down for several days in a battle with three Soviet infantry divisions.

At this point Nazi politics and pride entered the tactical equation, and threw a massive spanner in the works of Manstein's counteroffensive. Stung by his ungraceful departure from Kharkov three weeks earlier, Hausser was determined not to allow the army to share in the glory of recapturing his prize. In direct disobedience of orders to keep his tanks out of the city, Hausser planned to send the *Das Reich* Division into Kharkov from the west, while the *Leibstandarte* Division pushed in from the north. The *Totenkopf* Division was to continue its original mission to encircle the city.

> *For five days the Waffen-SS men battled through fanatical resistance in the concrete high-rise blocks*

For five days the Waffen-SS men battled through fanatical resistance in the concrete high-rise housing blocks that dominated the approaches to the city centre. The remnants of the Soviet Third Tank Army, reinforced by armed citizens, fought for every street and building.

By 10 March the *Totenkopf* and *Leibstandarte* had cleared the town of Dergachi, 16km (10 miles) to the north of Kharkov, of Soviet defenders, opening the way for the *Leibstandarte* to swing southwards down two main roads into the heart of the city. Two large kampfgruppen were formed, based around each of the division's panzergrenadier regiments, for the assault operation and they were reinforced with strong assault gun, 88mm flak gun and Nebelwefer rocket launcher support. A third kampfgruppe made up of the reconnaissance battalion and a panzer battalion, led by Meyer, was to push farther eastwards and then enter Kharkov to close the escape route of the

■ *Below:* Waffen-SS tank crews rearm their Panzer IVs during a pause in Manstein's counteroffensive.

defenders. This took him through a heavily wooded and swampy region, which required plenty of guile and cunning to safely navigate. The column got hopelessly disorganized in the woods, as the tanks were pressed into service to drag bogged-down reconnaissance jeeps out of the mud caused by an early thaw. Meyer, of course, was at the head of the column and, as he emerged from the forest, a large Soviet infantry regiment blocked his path. Fortunately, a roving Stuka patrol intervened and devastated the Russian column.

The Soviets rushed reinforcements, including a tank brigade and an élite brigade of NKVD security troops, into the city to try to set up an improvised defence line. Hausser was determined not to let the Russians build up their strength, so the *Leibstandarte* and *Das Reich* Divisions were ordered to press on with a night assault during the early hours of 11 March. The two main *Leibstandarte* assaults immediately ran into heavy resistance, backed by tank counterattacks all along the northern edge of the city. Assault guns were brought up to deal with the enemy tanks, but a vicious duel developed during the day with many Waffen-SS vehicles being put out of action. Progress could only be made with the support of the Nebelwerfer rocket launchers, but even then no breakthrough was achieved.

The key attack, as always, was led by Meyer. With his small column of motorcycles, jeeps, halftracks, two Marder self-propelled antitank guns and nine tanks, he set off in darkness to raid the city. His kampfgruppe weaved its way past a number of Soviet positions, until a pair of T-34s spotted it and opened fire, destroying a panzer. In the confusion, a Soviet antitank crew opened fire and destroyed their own tanks, inadvertently clearing the way for Meyer. He then pressed his column on into the city and it had reached the cemetery by midday,

■ *Below:* A platoon of Panzer IVs mount up before heading out of their forward base in a snow-covered Ukrainian village to engage a Soviet tank column.

but then had to halt when its tanks ran out of fuel. It then formed an all-round defensive position and waited for relief. Meyer's force was besieged in the cemetery overnight by thousands of Russian troops and armed civilians. The Germans furiously dug in to escape the effects of mortar and artillery fire that was raking their positions.

Hausser now received orders instructing him to call off the attack by *Das Reich*'s *Der Führer* Regiment, but the Waffen-SS commander ignored them. The battle continued to rage in the city throughout the night. To the west, the *Leibstandarte*'s two panzergrenadier regiments began their advance again, this time supported by panzers and 88mm flak guns in the front-assault echelons. Snipers in high-rise flats were blasted with quad

*Snipers in high-rise flats were blasted with quad 20mm flak cannon mounted on halftracks*

20mm flak cannon mounted on halftracks, while the panzers and flak guns defeated Soviet counterattacks by roving groups of T-34s. The *Leibstandarte*'s Tigers spearheaded the attacks, acting as mobile "pillboxes". The armoured monsters could park on street corners and dominate whole city blocks, while being impervious to enemy fire of all types.

Later in the day, Joachim Peiper's armoured personnel carrier battalion was at last able to break through the Red defence to established a tenuous link with the impetuous Meyer trapped in the cemetery. It brought in much-needed ammunition and fuel, before evacuating the wounded. Meyer's depleted kampfgruppe had to remain in position to block any moves by the Russians to reinforce their defences in the centre of the city.

■ *Above:* Luftwaffe Stuka dive-bombers operated from improvised airfields to ensure Waffen-SS tank columns had continuous air support during the advance on Kharkov in early 1943.

■ *Left:* Forward air controllers working with Waffen-SS panzer columns were able to call upon Luftwaffe aircraft to deal with any pockets of Soviet resistance encountered.

During the night and into the next day, several Waffen-SS kampfgruppen swept through central Kharkov. Every block had to be cleared of snipers, dug-in antitank guns and lone T-34 tanks. The *Leibstandarte* commanders drove their men forward into attack after attack to prevent the Soviets reorganizing their defence. The *Der Führer* Regiment continued to press in from the west to add to the pressure on the Russians in the tractor factory area in eastern Kharkov. The bulk of the *Das Reich* Division was pushing south of the city to cut through large Soviet defensive positions and complete the German ring around the city. *Das Reich*'s tanks cleared a key hill to the southeast of Kharkov on 14 March, destroying 29 antitank guns and scores of bunkers, to break the back of Soviet resistance.

Within the city, the Soviet defenders were still putting up a tenacious resistance.

> *Resistance from the population was intense, and thousands of Kharkov's citizens joined in the battle*

They quickly withdrew from threatened areas, and then used the sewers and ruins to move in behind the Waffen-SS troops. Peiper's armoured halftrack battalion proved invaluable because of its relative invulnerability to rifle fire from the scores of Soviet snipers who were still at large in areas "cleared" by the *Leibstandarte*. Resistance from the population was intense, and thousands of Kharkov's citizens joined in the battle to prevent their city becoming part of the Third Reich again.

The brutal nature of the fighting in Kharkov was emphasized by the fact that more than 1000 Waffen-SS men were killed or wounded. On 14 March the operation to seize the city was complete, and German radio began issuing gloating bulletins about the Soviet defeat. At the Führer's headquarters in East Prussia, plans were being made for a bumper issue of medals to the "heroes" of I SS Panzer Corps.

The main group of Soviet forces in the city was now pulling back southwards into the face of the advancing XXXXVIII Panzer Corps. There was now the possibility of the Germans catching elements of more than 10 enemy divisions and tank corps in a pocket.

On 13 March the *Totenkopf* Division completed its wide sweep north of Kharkov, with SS-Obersturmbannführer Otto Baum's panzergrenadier regiment, backed by a panzer battalion, capturing the Donets crossing at Chuguyev to seal the noose around Rybalko and his men. The *Totenkopf* attack punched south and eastwards to link up with the 6th Panzer Division advancing northeastwards. The *Das Reich, Totenkopf*, 6th Panzer and 11th Panzer Divisions then proceeded to chop-up the huge Soviet force hiding in the pocket south of Kharkov. Stalin gave Rybalko permission to give up the defence of the city and break out to the east. The trapped Russians made desperate efforts to escape, staging massive human-wave assaults to break past the *Totenkopf*'s blocking positions along the Donets.

The German noose was not pulled tight enough, and five days later the remnants of the Third Tank Army completed their break-out past Chuguyev, which was then held by weak army panzer divisions. Unlike Hitler, Stalin realized the importance of getting skilled troops out of pockets rather than leaving them to their fate (Rybalko survived the ordeal and went on to command his army with distinction at Kursk during the summer). The exposed *Totenkopf* Division would have been in real trouble if the Soviets had tried to break through to the forces trapped near Kharkov with their reserve Guards tank corps, but it was held back to secure the north Donets line.

To complete the German victory, Hausser dashed panzer kampfgruppen north to link up with the *Grossdeutschland* Division, which had been taking on Soviet armoured units defending Belgorod. An unofficial "race" developed between the *Leibstandarte* and the élite army division for the honour of seizing the last major centre of Soviet resistance in the Ukraine.

The first line of Soviet resistance, some 16km (10 miles) north of Kharkov, was rolled over on 16 March by the *Leibstandarte*'s 2nd Panzergrenadier Regiment, supported by a huge barrage of Nebelwerfer and artillery fire, as well as wave after wave of Stuka dive-bombers. A line of Soviet antitank guns and infantry bunkers ceased to exist. Next day, Peiper's kampfgruppe was unleashed northwards

■ *Below:* A Waffen-SS Panzer IV watches over a German patrol as it moves into the outskirts of Kharkov in early March 1943, during the operation to encircle the bastion of Soviet resistance in the Ukraine.

with strong armoured support, including the *Leibstandarte*'s Tiger detachment. This powerful force made easy meat of another enemy antitank gun position during the afternoon.

After a pause during the night to rearm and organize air support, Peiper was off again. On cue, more Stukas attacked a large road-block just after dawn on the morning of 18 March. With the road now clear, Peiper ordered his armoured force forward again. He did not stop until his tanks and armoured carriers were in the centre of Belgorod at 11.35 hours. Eight T-34s encountered on the drive north were destroyed by the Tigers – all other Soviet positions had been ignored. "Sepp" Dietrich flew north in his Storch aircraft to congratulate Peiper on his success. The German *coup de main* operation may have taken the

■ *Above:* Soviet infantry and partisans put up fanatical resistance against Waffen-SS troops from the high-rise blocks of flats on the northern outskirts of Kharkov.

■ *Left:* SS-Obersturmbann-führer Fritz Witt, commander of the *Leibstandarte*'s panzergrenadier regiment, points out Soviet positions to a subordinate during the assault on Kharkov.

Russians by surprise, but during the afternoon they pulled themselves together and launched a string of armoured counterattacks. The *Leibstandarte*'s panzers repulsed all the attacks, destroying 14 tanks, 38 trucks and 16 antitank guns.

It was not until later in the afternoon, however, when the *Das Reich*'s *Deutschland* Panzergrenadier Regiment linked up with Peiper's kampfgruppe, that the German position in the town was fully secure. The Russians continued to harry Peiper's men in the town, and he was forced to conduct a number of panzer sweeps of the countryside to expand the German grip on the region. During one such operation a pair of Tiger I tanks were attacked by Russian tanks, who destroyed an accompanying armoured halftrack before they were driven off for the loss of 10 tanks, two armoured cars and 10 trucks.

Peiper's dash to Belgorod had been possible thanks to a return of winter weather, but in the final days of March the temperature was rising and the snow disappeared. It was replaced by deep mud, which made all movement off roads, even by tracked vehicles, almost impossible. The *Totenkopf* and *Das Reich* Divisions fought a series of bitter infantry battles to establish a firm frontline along the Donets, east of Kharkov, for several days, but the spring campaign season was all but over.

Back in Kharkov, Waffen-SS panzergrenadiers combed the ruins of the city for the few remaining pockets of Soviet troops, and were also settling some old scores with its citizens. The desecration of the graves of Waffen-SS men killed during the January battles, and the mutilation of the bodies, made the *Leibstandarte* very loath to show any quarter to captured Russian soldiers.

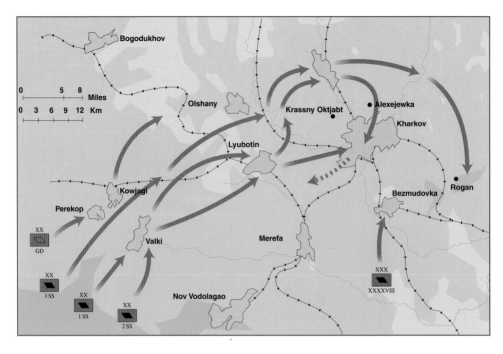

■ *Above:* Offensive operations of the *Grossdeutschland* Division, I SS Panzer Corps and XXXXVIII Panzer Corps against Kharkov, 7–10 March 1943.

■ *Left:* A Waffen-SS MG 42 machine-gun team clears out Soviet troops from a factory complex in the south of Kharkov.

Several hundred wounded Soviet soldiers were murdered when Dietrich's men occupied the city's military hospital. Any captured commissars or senior Russian officers were executed as a matter of routine, in line with Hitler's infamous "commissar order".

Special German Gestapo squads, SS Sonderkommando security units and Einsatzgruppen with mobile gas chambers followed close behind the victorious German troops, to ensure there was no repeat of February's uprising. An estimated 10,000 men, women and children perished during Hausser's short reign of terror in the city of Kharkov.

On 18 March, the German High Command claimed that 50,000 Russian soldiers had died during Manstein's counteroffensive, along with 19,594 taken prisoner and 1140 tanks and 3000 guns destroyed.

An impressive total but, when compared to the 250,000 Germans lost at Stalingrad, it is clear that the Soviets benefited more from the Kharkov battles. The Russians, their military production in full swing, could also replace their losses more easily.

I SS Panzer Corps played a key part in this victory. It demonstrated that it was one of the world's foremost armoured formations, holding out against superior odds and then counterattacking with great skill and *élan*. Its success was not achieved cheaply, though. Some 11,500 Waffen-SS men were killed or wounded during the two-month campaign in the Ukraine. Some 4500 of these were borne by the *Leibstandarte*, emphasizing its key role at the centre of all the major battles of the campaign. Indeed, the majority of the casualties were in the combat units of the three Waffen-SS divi-

■ *Below:* A German StuG III crew inspect their kill – a Soviet T-34/76. They are trying to prise open the hatch to kill the crew who remain inside.

■ *Left:* Kharkov burns. The city was the scene of brutal fighting for over a week. The result was thousands of its civilians killed and even more made homeless.

sions. Not to be forgotten is the role of the *Wiking* Division serving with the First Panzer Army. It lost thousands of men in a series of small skirmishes, but was still able to take the offensive and defeat superior odds. The material strength of I SS Panzer Corps was badly affected by two months of battle. Its panzer regiments could only field less than half the number of tanks they had brought from France eight weeks before.

Manstein was justifiably dubbed "the saviour of the Eastern Front" for his efforts in turning back the Russian tide. Events later in the year would prove the Red Army's defeat was only a temporary setback. The antics of the Waffen-SS in Kharkov placed the final phase of the German counteroffensive under a cloud. Hausser's premature assault cost his corps thousands of casualties and allowed the Third Tank Army to escape through the weak German encirclement force. The butchery of the Waffen-SS after they broke into the city was not really remarkable – it was standard behaviour for a

■ *Left:* *Leibstandarte* Division panzergrenadiers patrol through the ruins of Kharkov – with tank support – looking for Soviet stragglers.

force that was in the vanguard of their Führer's murderous campaign to rid Europe of Jews and Bolsheviks.

This, of course, was irrelevant to Hitler, who in the weeks after Kharkov expressed a faith in the élite Waffen-SS divisions that knew no bounds. He declared I SS Panzer Corps to be "worth 20 Italian divisions". Of more importance to those divisions, though, was the Führer's express order to General Zeitzler, his Army Chief of Staff, that "we must see that the SS gets the necessary personnel". And, in preparation for the summer campaign season, they were also to be given priority when it came to delivery of the latest Panzer V Panther tanks, much to the annoyance of the army.

A combination of mud and exhaustion brought military operations to a halt on the Eastern Front in mid-March 1943. Both sides needed to reorganize and re-equip for the forthcoming campaign season.

■ *Below:* A *Leibstandarte* tank column pauses before entering the maelstrom that is Kharkov. The obsolete Panzer II tanks were used for liaison and reconnaissance tasks at this stage in the war.

# CHAPTER 2

# KURSK

## II SS Panzer Corps during Operation Citadel, July 1943.

During July 1943, the eyes of the world were on a nondescript stretch of undulating steppe around the previously unknown Russian city of Kursk. The run-down and unremarkable city, however, would soon enter military history as the centre point of the most decisive battle of World War II. Here, the might of the German Wehrmacht would stage its last major strategic offensive of the war on the Eastern Front. The Red Army held its ground, and within weeks would stage its own massive counteroffensive that eventually drove all the way to the heart of the Third Reich, to Berlin itself. After Kursk, Stalin's armies would hold the strategic initiative on the Eastern Front.

In the build-up to the battle both sides massed their best troops, tanks, artillery and aircraft. By early July, the Germans had concentrated 43 divisions, with 2700 tanks and assault guns, supported by 1800 combat aircraft. Barring their way were 100 Russian divisions and five tank armies, with 3306 tanks and 2650 aircraft. Within days these gigantic war machines would clash to decide the fate of the world.

The origins of this titanic clash stretched back to the winter battles around Kharkov in February and March 1943. German counterattacks pushed back the Soviet spearheads that had surged westwards during the winter. By the time the spring thaw made all movement off roads impossible, the Wehrmacht had regained lost ground and stabilized the front. But the Soviets retained control of a huge salient that bulged more than 80km (50 miles) westwards into German-held territory.

To the German High Command, the 160km- (100-mile-) wide salient was a prize that could not be resisted. A rapid panzer advance,

■ **Left:** A *Das Reich* Division Tiger I tank moves forward at Kursk as Waffen-SS panzergrenadiers consolidate their positions on the exposed Russian steppe.

punching inwards from either shoulder of the salient, would trap hundreds of thousands of Russian troops and, in turn, shorten the German front. This would free more than 15 divisions and allow a new offensive to be mounted on the Eastern Front, one that would finally finish off Stalin's resistance once and for all. For Adolf Hitler, the proposed Kursk Offensive offered a chance to turn the tide of war in Germany's favour to counter growing Anglo-American power in the West (the campaign in North Africa had ended in Axis defeat in May 1943). If Russia could be defeated, then the might of the Wehrmacht could be turned westwards in time for the expected cross-Channel invasion in 1944. German success on the Eastern Front was also seen by the Führer as an essential gambit to keep key Axis allies – Romania, Hungary, Italy and Finland – fighting on Berlin's side. Hitler was also convinced that the raw materials and industrial resources of the Ukraine would be decisive in the "war of production" between the Axis and the Allies.

Hitler's generals were divided concerning how to proceed. His field commanders in the East wanted an immediate offensive in April, to exploit their victories around

■ *Above:* Field Marshal Erich von Manstein, Army Group South's tactical genius, surveys the Russian frontline in the tense days before the start of Operation Citadel.

■ *Right:* Marder III self-propelled anti-tank guns combined Czech tank chassis with captured Russian 76.2mm antitank guns to produce a potent tank killer for the Waffen-SS.

Kharkov and catch the Soviets before they had time to rebuild their strength. Others wanted to husband the precious panzer divisions and use them to launch a decisive counterstroke against the expected Soviet summer offensive, to capitalize on the Wehrmacht's experience and expertise in armoured warfare.

The Führer was at first undecided. As ever, he was keen to attack, but wanted any offensive to be a dramatic success which would signal that Germany was still the dominant military power in the world. For this reason he was determined to use Germany's newest "wonder weapons" to inflict a punishing defeat on the Red Army. The new 45.72-tonne (45-ton) Panzer V Panther tank and Ferdinand super-heavy assault guns/tank destroyers

were to spearhead the attack. Hitler placed great store on the Panther, and repeatedly delayed the offensive to ensure that large numbers of the new tank would be ready to spearhead the assault operation. While preparations for the offensive began in April, it was not until the first days of July that Hitler gave the go-ahead.

The plan's strategic concept was essentially very simple. Colonel-General Walter Model's Ninth Army was to push southwards into the northern shoulder of the salient. At the same time, Field Marshal Erich von Manstein's Army Group South would strike northwards to link up with Model's men, trapping the Soviet defenders holding the line west of Kursk. Both attack forces were to contain strong armoured reserves, which would be

*While preparations for the offensive began in April, it was not until July that Hitler gave the go-ahead*

■ *Above:* **Sturmgeschütz (StuG) III assault guns combined with Tiger I tanks to blast a path through Soviet defences for Waffen-SS panzergrenadiers.**

on hand to defeat any Russian counter-attacks. Operation Citadel was to be a repeat of the classic Blitzkrieg victories of 1941–42, when huge Soviet armies had been encircled with ease by marauding panzer armies.

Model's assault force eventually grew to include some six army panzer divisions, two panzergrenadier divisions and 13 infantry divisions. Two battalions of the monster Ferdinands would spearhead an assault force that contained more than 700 tanks and 250 assault guns.

The most powerful elements of the German attack force, however, were concentrated on the southern axis, where Manstein had three army panzer corps and three infantry corps. He also had command of II SS Panzer Corps, which had grown into the most powerful tank formation on the European mainland, with 430 tanks and assault guns ready for action on the eve of battle. III and XXXXVIII Panzer Corps, of

the Fourth Panzer Army, boasted more than 870 tanks and assault guns at the start of Operation Citadel, the codename of the German offensive. In reserve was XXIV Panzer Corps with another 150 tanks. In total, Manstein had amassed some 1500 armoured vehicles for the attack, including the first 200 Panthers which were formed into a special brigade to support the Army's *Grossdeutschland* Panzergrenadier Division.

The Luftwaffe built up a major force of tank-hunting aircraft to provide close air support to the assault troops. These assets included 37mm cannon-armed Junkers Ju 87G Stukas and 30mm cannon-armed Henschel Hs 129s. Manstein had more than 1000 Luftwaffe combat aircraft to support his offensive, and a string of radar stations were positioned around the southern flank of the salient to give prior warning of Russian air activity.

The surrender of 230,000 German troops in Tunisia in May to British and

> *In total, Manstein had amassed some 1500 armoured vehicles for the attack*

■ *Below:* The Leibstandarte Division's single Tiger I company destroyed hundreds of Soviet tanks and antitank guns during the 10 days the division was committed to Operation Citadel.

■ *Above:* Tiger tank crews had to spend almost all their spare time ensuring their vehicles were running at their optimum efficiency.

who wanted to build up his beloved Waffen-SS so he would not have to rely on the army and its generals, who in his mind only seemed to want to retreat.

At the end of March, the Führer informed the *Leibstandarte* Division's commander, SS-Obergruppenführer Josef "Sepp" Dietrich, that his unit would be the core of a new corps, to be known as I SS Panzer Corps *Leibstandarte Adolf Hitler*. Scores of staff officer from Dietrich's division would form the new corps staff, while hundreds of officers and noncommissioned officers were to be drafted to form a training cadre to establish the new Hitler Youth SS panzergrenadier division. A number of artillery, assault gun and antitank battalions were also transferred from the *Leibstandarte* to the new division, to provide the core of its specialist regiments.

As a result of these developments, Hausser's formation was renamed II SS Panzer Corps, even though it was the first such headquarters to be set up by the Waffen-SS.

## Preparations for the offensive

As trainloads of *Leibstandarte* veterans headed westwards, those who remained behind were ordered to prepare their units for action in a few weeks' time. Thousands of replacement soldiers were now arriving on a daily basis. These were mostly a mix of raw conscripts and drafted Luftwaffe ground personnel. Gone were the days when the Waffen-SS could pick and choose who served in its ranks. When Dietrich greeted the first batch of ex-Luftwaffe men in Kharkov, he asked for volunteers for the panzergrenadiers. There were few takers – most of the new Waffen-SS men wanted to serve in maintenance and repair teams. In future the replacements were not to be given a choice regarding which units they would serve in. Most of these recruits were directed to the *Leibstandarte* Division because of the heavy casualties it had suffered during the previous two months.

American forces stiffened Hitler's resolve to launch Operation Citadel. In his mind there was no time to spare before Anglo-American forces made landings on mainland Europe.

During the final days of March 1943, SS-Obergruppenführer Paul Hausser was able to finally pull his weary divisions out of the line to be rested and rebuilt. The *Leibstandarte*, *Das Reich* and *Totenkopf* Divisions were pulled back to billets in Kharkov and neighbouring towns, which only a few months before had been battlegrounds. There was little in the way of home comforts, but the Waffen-SS men had other things on their minds. A major reorganization of the corps was ordered by the Führer,

A constant stream of trains arrived at Kharkov with new tanks, artillery, vehicles and other equipment. Waffen-SS repair teams worked overtime to restore the scores of tanks damaged in action back to fighting condition. No one trusted them to be returned in time for the coming offensive if they were shipped back to workshops in Germany.

The panzer regiments of the Waffen-SS divisions were extensively reorganized to absorb their new equipment. The *Leibstandarte* and *Das Reich* Divisions were both ordered to send the first battalion of their panzer regiments back to Germany, for training in the use of the new Panther tank. This process would not be complete by the time Operation Citadel began, contrary to the many accounts of the Battle of Kursk which have stated that the Waffen-SS divisions fielded hundreds of the new tanks during the offensive. In fact, the Panther would not make its appearance on the Eastern Front in Waffen-SS service until the middle of August 1943.

The Waffen-SS was also not equipped with hundreds of Tiger I tanks at Kursk: only three companies of the heavy tanks saw service with II SS Panzer Corps during July 1943. Each division did have a battalion of Sturmgeschütz (StuG) III assault guns and a strong contingent of Marder III self-propelled antitank guns.

By the time Operation Citadel got under way, the *Leibstandarte*'s panzer regi-

■ *Below:* SdKfz 250 halftracks and Panzer III tanks manoeuvre on the steppe in the run-up to a combined-arms attack during the Kursk Offensive.

ment boasted one battalion, with 67 Panzer IV and 13 Panzer III tanks, along with 13 Tiger Is. The *Das Reich* Division was less well equipped, with only 33 Panzer IVs, 62 Panzer IIIs and 14 Tiger Is. To boost its fighting power, the division pressed 25 captured T-34s into service. The *Totenkopf* Division still had two battalions in its panzer regiment, but 63 of its tanks were Panzer IIIs. It also had 44 heavier Panzer IVs and 15 Tiger Is.

The *Wiking* Division's panzer unit had been upgraded to regimental status, however it had yet to grow beyond battalion strength. In July 1943 it could only muster 23 Panzer III and 17 Panzer IV tanks. It had no Tigers, and was kept in reserve throughout the Kursk Offensive.

To further increase the firepower of Hausser's corps, the army provided two heavy artillery and two rocket launcher regiments, as well as a special command headquarters to coordinate fire missions of all artillery units in the corps. This meant that huge amounts of firepower could be brought down on individual targets in a very short space of time.

To prepare his command for battle, Hausser ordered a series of training exercises to be held. Noncommissioned officers

drilled the new recruits to turn them into combat soldiers. Tank driving and gunnery courses were run on the new vehicles and weapons being delivered to the Waffen-SS. Senior commanders were given top-secret briefings on the Operation Citadel plan, and were shown scores of Luftwaffe aerial photographs of the Soviet defences in their respective sectors.

Company and battalion field exercises were held on the steppe around Kharkov to familiarize the troops with equipment and practice the tactics to be used during the coming battle. Finally, divisional and corps "command post" exercises were put on to acquaint the Waffen-SS commanders and staff officers with the plan. They based their planning on intelligence that said four Russian infantry divisions

*Tank driving and gunnery courses were run on the new vehicles and weapons being delivered*

were holding the enemy's first defensive line in II SS Panzer Corps' sector. Two more held the second line, and behind them were two tank corps with at least 360 tanks. After defeating these forces, counterattacks were to be expected from several more enemy tank corps. Although many Waffen-SS men were superbly confident regarding their own equipment and abilities – arrogance was a common trait among Hitler's "master race" – some of the older veterans knew the coming battle would be like no other they had previously faced.

By the end of June, II SS Panzer Corps was warned to be ready to move forward to its assembly area in a few days. The Führer decided on 21 June – almost two years to the day since the start of his invasion of Russia – to launch the operation on 5 July.

■ *Above:* A *Das Reich* Division Panzer IV during Operation Citadel. This vehicle is equipped with the short-barrelled 75mm cannon.

On 1 July Hitler called his senior commanders to his headquarters in East Prussia to receive a final "pep talk". There was now no turning back. The Waffen-SS divisions started to move from their billets around Kharkov to their assembly areas near Belgorod in a series of night-time road moves. During daylight hours they remained out of sight in forests, waiting for X-Day, as the start day of the operation was codenamed, to dawn.

On the other side of the frontline, Marshal of the Soviet Union Georgi Zhukov was ready and waiting for the German offensive. The victor of the battles of Moscow and Stalingrad also recognized the importance of the Kursk salient, and was not prepared to give it up lightly. He knew the Germans would attack, and saw the chance to engage their precious panzer divisions in a war of attrition. Once they had been worn down, he would launch his reserves in a massive offensive along the whole length of the Eastern Front, to inflict

a strategic defeat of such magnitude that the Third Reich would not be able to recover.

Zhukov was appointed personally to coordinate the defence of Kursk, and he was given unlimited resources to do the job. Unknown to the Soviet commander, his biggest help came from his British allies, who for three years had been reading all of the Third Reich's secret radio communications traffic. The British had broken the Germans' Enigma code using an early form of computer, but they were unwilling to reveal to Stalin the full extent of their code-breaking success, and so created a convoluted means to pass so-called "Ultra" material to Moscow. This involved establishing contact with a ring of Soviet agents in Switzerland, codenamed Lucy, and drip-feeding them Ultra decodes relevant to the war in Russia. The Lucy agents were convinced they were receiving documents from disgruntled German officers within Hitler's inner circle. The result was that within days Moscow had verbatim transcripts of high-

■ *Below:* A *Totenkopf* Division Panzer III platoon moves through a Russian village during the early phase of Operation Citadel.

level orders being sent from Hitler's headquarters to his senior commanders on the Eastern Front. These included all the plans for Operation Citadel, including details of units, objectives, logistic information and, most crucially, the date for the start of the offensive. Hitler's desire to micro-manage the war down to the lowest level played into the Soviets' hands. They knew the every move of almost all German units, often before the commanders of those units themselves. Indeed, Manstein's success during the Kharkov Offensive has been attributed to the fact that he did not consult the Führer on many of his moves, so they were not compromised to the Lucy Ring and thus caught Red Army commanders by surprise.

With this vital information in his hip pocket, Zhukov was able to plan his defence in a methodical way. Nothing would be left to chance. The key to Zhukov's plan was the need to prevent the German panzers from breaking free and manoeuvring against the Soviet rear areas. He recognized that Soviet units were inferior to the Germans when it came to mobile warfare, and he wanted to close down the battle into a series of local set-piece actions. A network of strongpoints, each reinforced with scores of antitank guns, were built around the Kursk salient. Each strong-point was mutually supporting, so once the Germans attacked one they would be raked by well-aimed fire from another. The Germans were to be given no chance to put their mobile Blitzkrieg tactics into action, especially rampaging into the rear of Soviet formations and positions. Zhukov wanted to capitalize on his soldiers' dogged determination in defensive operations. He wanted to trade their lives and their antitank guns for panzers. Russia had a massive supply of men and hardware at this stage of the war, while Germany could never hope to replace its panzer divisions, which had been rebuilt after the disaster at Stalingrad, if they were decimated once more. This was to be the

> *The Germans were to be given no chance to put their mobile Blitzkrieg tactics into action*

■ *Above:* Contrary to popular legend, the famous Panther tank did not see action with II SS Panzer Corps during Operation Citadel. The only unit to use the Panther at Kursk was the Army's *Grossdeutschland* Panzergrenadier Division.

Verdun of the Eastern Front – a brutal battle of attrition rather than a fast-moving tank battle.

For three months the Russians poured men and machines into the Kursk salient to build a string of defence lines almost 48km (30 miles) deep. Millions of mines were laid along the length of the salient, and behind them thousands of antitank guns and artillery pieces were sited in hundreds of strongpoints. Positioned between the defence lines were tank brigades, ready to launch immediate counterattacks, and behind the four main defence lines were tank corps held in reserve to seal any German breakthroughs. Hundreds of kilometres to the rear was the Fifth Guards Tank Army, Zhukov's strategic reserve, which was being held ready to deliver the *coup de grâce* against the German offensive. Once committed, the Soviet strategic reserve would decide the fate of the war on the Eastern Front.

*The Soviet Sixth Guards Army created what was intended to be a death trap for the Waffen-SS men*

In II SS Panzer Corps' sector, the Soviet Sixth Guards Army created what was intended to be a death trap for the Waffen-SS men. Facing the brunt of the German attack were the soldiers of the 67th and 52nd Guards Rifle Divisions. They manned a series of strongpoints along a ridge line, which allowed them to observe the approach routes to the southern shoulder of the Kursk salient and call down massive barrages of artillery and multi-barrel Katyusha rocket launcher (the so-called Stalin's Organ) fire on German assembly areas. Two antitank regiments and two tank regiments were spread out among the first-echelon divisions to stiffen their resistance. The tanks and antitank guns were emplaced in bunkers to protect them from shell fire. Along the front was some 290km (181

■ *Above:* Marshal of the Soviet Union Georgi Zhukov masterminded the Soviet defence of the Kursk salient during the critical days in July 1943.

miles) of trench lines. Hundreds of kilometres of antitank ditches were dug to channel the German attack towards antitank killing zones. More than 1000 machine-gun nests and mortar batteries were positioned to cover the mine belts, to stop German combat engineers clearing paths through the 140,000 mines. Some 300 pillboxes and over 3000 individual bunkers protected several thousand riflemen and tank-hunting squads armed with antitank rifles. Some

9.6km (six miles) behind the main defence line were three infantry divisions, a tank brigade and two more regiments of antitank guns. They had prepared similarly strong defence lines to their comrades in the front-line, although the mine belts were thinner with only 30,000 mines. Throughout the Sixth Guards Army's sector, there were more than 400 antitank guns between 45mm and 76mm calibre, some 778 mortars and almost 500 artillery pieces between 76mm

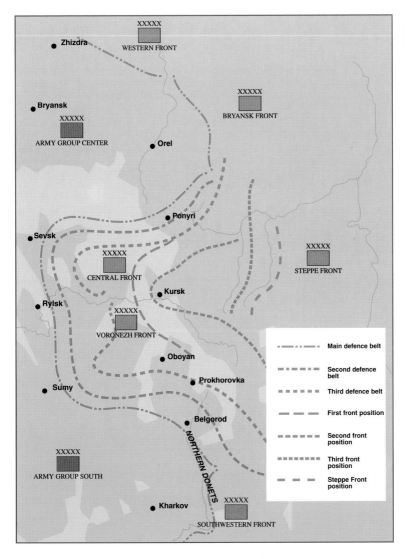

■ *Left:* Soviet defensive belts in the Kursk salient, July 1943.

■ *Above:* Behind the Soviet front were more than 3000 tanks – the majority T-34/76s – ready to counter-attack any German breakthrough.

contained a far higher density of mines, machine guns, mortars and antitank guns than in the second line. Not content with this density of fortification, Zhukov ordered another defensive sector – of three lines – to be build at the base of salient, in case the Germans punched through the initial defence lines. To add to the Germans' problems, all the construction work on the Soviet defensive positions was to be conducted at night or under camouflage nets so Luftwaffe photographic reconnaissance would not be able to pinpoint them. Hundreds of dummy trench lines, bunkers and minefields were also prepared to confuse German intelligence. When the Germans attacked they would have little idea of the real tactical layout of the Russian positions, beyond what they could see from their own trenches.

From the Lucy Ring reports and tactical intelligence from prisoners and deserters, Zhukov knew almost the hour when the German assault would begin. He seemed to hold all the cards. The wily Soviet commander, however, was far from complacent. Once the battle started he knew that anything could happen.

By the evening of 3 July, II SS Panzer Corps was deployed in its assembly areas and final orders were issued for the initial assault. On the left was the *Leibstandarte*, in the centre was *Das Reich* and the *Totenkopf* was deployed on the right. All were to attack

and 203mm calibre. They were all in prepared positions, and their target-spotting teams had had three months to pre-register ranges and targets.

Nearly 48km (30 miles) behind the front were the so-called rear-defence lines, which were sited on a number of key rivers, blocking the advance to Kursk itself. These

■ *Above:* In its sector alone, II SS Panzer Corps faced more than 400 Soviet 45mm- and 76mm-calibre antitank guns.

■ *Left:* The Soviet Fifth Guards Tank Army was held far behind the front as Zhukov's strategic reserve, to be committed only when the battle had reached its climax.

simultaneously to batter through the Russian defence lines.

The attack was to start just before midnight on the evening of 4 July, with battalion-sized infantry assaults going in to seize a number of key Soviet positions to allow artillery observers to be sited so they could call in fire to cover the attack against the main Russian defence line. Soviet artillery barrages started to fall on the Waffen-SS divisions' assembly areas just after dusk, causing minor casualties and confusion, but they were not intense enough to stop the main attack. The first attacks went in on schedule, with small groups of panzergrenadiers infiltrating through minefields and rushing the enemy trenches. In two hours of hand-to-hand combat, the outposts were captured and the main attack of the *Leibstandarte* Division

*Each of the division's panzergrenadier regiments was given a Russian strongpoint as an objective*

was ready to roll at just after dawn – 04:05 hours – on 5 July.

Each of the division's panzergrenadier regiments was given a major Russian strongpoint as an objective. The Waffen-SS panzer regiments and armoured troop-carrier battalions were kept in reserve to exploit any breakthrough created by the panzergrenadiers. For 50 minutes before the attack the massed artillery of the corps blasted the objectives, and in the final five minutes of the barrage Junkers Ju 87 Stuka dive-bombers joined the attack. The bombardment demolished whole sections of trench line and scores of antitank guns, stunning the Russian defenders. Once the *Leibstandarte*'s attack was under way, the artillery and Stuka support was switched to "soften up" the defences in front of the *Das Reich* Division, which was due to attack at 08:15 hours.

Tiger Is, StuG IIIs and Marders then rolled forward with the first wave of panzergrenadiers to give them close support as they moved into action. This was the so-called panzerkeil, or wedge, tactic. The presence of the armoured firepower was the key to the success of the assault, with the Tigers and other vehicles acting as mobile pillboxes. They destroyed scores of machine-gun nests in quick succession to allow the panzergrenadier assault teams to move in to clear out the trench lines with hand grenades and flamethrowers. Dozens of antitank guns were destroyed by the giant tanks, which were impervious to Soviet fire. These assault operations took until well into the afternoon, and cost the *Leibstandarte* Division some 500 casualties alone. The close-quarter fighting was vicious and few Soviet soldiers showed any inclination to surrender, with just over 100 being captured by the Waffen-SS during the day. By mid-afternoon, the *Leibstandarte* and *Das Reich* Divisions were ready to start the next phase of the operation: launching their panzer reserves forward. *Das Reich*'s panzers got

stuck in a previously undiscovered mine-field, and the *Leibstandarte*'s surged ahead until they ran into the pak-front of the Soviet 28th Anti-Tank Brigade. Two Tigers were damaged by the expertly dug-in anti-tank guns, before the *Leibstandarte*'s commanders ordered the advance halted until infantry could be brought up during the night to clear out the enemy's second-line defences.

The *Leibstandarte* and *Das Reich* Divisions were the most successful units on the German southern wing on the first day of the offensive. Their army comrades on each wing got bogged down in the thick mud and the numerous Soviet minefields.

Throughout the night, the Waffen-SS commanders reorganized their forces to punch through the second line of enemy defences as soon as it got light. Again a massive artillery and rocket launcher bombardment was planned, to be followed by an infantry assault with Tiger tank support. It took almost two hours for the *Leibstandarte*'s panzergrenadiers to clear paths through the Soviet mine belts and

blow holes in the barbed-wire entanglements. Daylight came, and in four more hours of fighting the Waffen-SS men cleared out the enemy bunkers and gun positions.

Meanwhile, the *Das Reich*'s *Der Führer* Panzergrenadier Regiment was repulsed with heavy losses when it tried to take a strong-point in its sector. A divisional-sized artillery fire mission was needed to clear the way forward.

SS-Standartenführer Theodor Wisch, the *Leibstandarte*'s new commander, was forward in his armoured halftrack watching the battle, and once the panzergrenadiers had cleared a passage through the enemy position he gave orders for his panzer kampfgruppe to motor northwards. It had

barely moved a few hundred metres forward when more than 45 T-34s charged out of a wood directly at the Waffen-SS tanks. Eight were knocked out by the panzers, while Stuka dive-bombers picked off another three before the Soviet tanks retreated. The panzers were rearmed and refuelled in the forward battle zone from halftrack supply vehicles before moving forward again later in the afternoon, with panzergrenadiers providing support in armoured carriers. They only got a few kilometres northwards before the force ran into a massive pak-front and huge minefield. Four tanks and many halftracks were lost to mines. At the same time as the *Leibstandarte* Division's panzers were rolling forward, *Das Reich*'s panzer

kampfgruppe and reconnaissance battalion were ordered to exploit the breach created by their own panzergrenadiers. They destroyed 10 Soviet tanks, but were stropped in their tracks by antitank fire which hit a number of Tigers. Again the Soviets had managed to halt the German attack and prevent the panzers breaking into the open countryside.

Out on the Waffen-SS right flank, the *Totenkopf* Division was still battling to cut through the 52nd Guards Rifle Division, which was tenaciously holding its main defence position during most of the morning. Attacks in the late morning broke the back of the defence, though, and the *Totenkopf* was able to make big gains. However, in the afternoon large Soviet counterattacks by II Guards Tank Corps battered the division's right flank. Wave after wave of tanks surged forward, with some attacks involving more than 300 Soviet tanks.

During the night of 6 July, the Russians reinforced V Guards Tank Corps opposite with three brigades in preparation for a major counterattack against the Waffen-SS. Small probing attacks were launched in the dawn light by individual tanks, supported by squads of tank-riding infantry. At 06:00

hours the *Leibstandarte* and *Das Reich* panzer kampfgruppen were ordered forward. In the morning gloom Soviet tank brigades attacked the Waffen-SS panzers from three sides. They surged forward in waves, to be hit by a wall of fire from the German panzers. The main assault wave was made up of dozens of T-34s. They were picked off one-by-one by the panzers, but still kept attacking. The *Leibstandarte*'s Tiger company was in the thick of the action, alone accounting for more than 30 T-34s.

In spite of their terrible losses, the Soviet tanks were soon among the German formations. Panzergrenadiers picked off those tanks that came close and shot any tank-riding infantry on their hulls. The battle raged all day. More than 90 tanks and 60 artillery pieces were lost and 600 Russians were captured in the battle, which decimated XXXI Tank Corps and III Mechanized Corps. Their actions, however, successfully blocked the German advance into the heart of the Soviet third defence line.

The tank dogfight between the Waffen-SS and Russian T-34 crews continued overnight and into the morning of 8 July. Soviet tank attacks were an almost hourly occurrence. Whole battalions and brigades

■ *Above:* 88mm flak guns provided a last line of defence against any stray Soviet tanks that broke through the thinly held sectors of the German front.

of T-34s would suddenly appear from forests and villages to charge the panzer kampfgruppen, which were at the tip of a 19.2km-(12-mile-) deep breach in Soviet lines gouged out by II SS Panzer Corps.

The *Leibstandarte* and *Das Reich* panzer kampfgruppen moved around the exposed steppe, destroying dozens of Soviet tanks with their long-range weapons. To increase the firepower available, the *Leibstandarte*'s assault gun battalion was moved up to the spearhead of the division.

The panzers and assault guns could not be everywhere, though, and individual Russians tanks easily penetrated the thinly stretched defences of the *Das Reich*'s and *Leibstandarte*'s panzergrenadier regiments. Antitank guns and hand grenades

*The* Leibstandarte *and* Das Reich *panzer kampfgruppen moved around the exposed steppe*

drove off most of the Russian attacks. Four T-34s managed to sneak through the German defences, and get within a few hundred metres of the *Leibstandarte*'s divisional headquarters, before they were knocked out by tank-hunting teams armed with hollow-charge mines.

Hausser was determined to press forward the attack, and so just before midday the *Leibstandarte* and *Das Reich* armoured kampfgruppen were ordered to wheel northwestwards. Their objective was to seize the crossings over the River Psel and breach the Russian third line, thus opening a clear route northwards.

The panzers, led by the *Leibstandarte*'s Tigers, destroyed 22 T-34s as they moved across the open steppe towards the river. As

■ *Above: Das Reich* Division StuG III assault guns move forward through an enemy artillery barrage on the exposed steppe at Kursk.

■ *Below:* Captured T-34/76 tanks being operated by the *Das Reich* Division take up their position in the German assault formation during the Kursk battles.

the assault groups approached the Psel valley, they ran into an antitank brigade hidden among the villages and woods along the valley. A network of mines and bunkers forced the panzer commanders to rein in their tanks. A small squad of *Das Reich*'s panzergrenadiers did score a major success when they infiltrated through a minefield and captured a Soviet divisional command post and a general. The Soviet defence did not crack, though, and the German drive north had been blocked.

Over on the eastern flank, the *Leibstandarte*'s assault gun battalion led a panzergrenadier attack northeastwards, which allowed several villages to be cleared of isolated pockets of Soviet infantry.

By the evening of 8 July, the two lead Waffen-SS divisions had destroyed more than 120 tanks, but 76 of their panzers were badly in need of repairs. Many of the panzer companies were down to half strength, and time was needed to patch up the scores of battle-damaged tanks that were filling up the repair workshops.

As the battle raged on at the schwerpunkt, Hausser put in train plans to relieve the *Totenkopf* Division and move it up to

punch a hole through the defences along the Psel. The *Totenkopf* Division had been holding the right flank of II SS Panzer Corps since the start of the offensive, and it spent most of the day handing over its sector to an army infantry division. The safe completion of this manoeuvre was only possible thanks to the intervention of the Luftwaffe. During the morning, three cannon-armed Hs 129 tank-hunting aircraft were patrolling to the east of the *Totenkopf*, when they spotted a Soviet tank brigade of 60 T-34s forming up ready to smash into the flank of the Waffen-SS corps. More aircraft were summoned and, in less than an hour, the whole brigade was destroyed by 30mm cannon fire, or forced to scatter into woods and gullies to hide from the aircraft. The attack totally disrupted the preparations of II Guards Tank Corps to pressurize the *Totenkopf*, allowing the Waffen-SS unit to successfully disengage from the front.

The first regiment of the *Totenkopf* Division was in position ready to attack the Psel line early after dawn on 9 July, along with the *Leibstandarte*'s 1st Panzergrenadier Regiment. It didn't have enough strength to punch through the heavily reinforced Soviet

■ *Below:* A *Totenkopf* Division tank and panzergrenadier column uses a valley to cover its advance as it moves towards the front.

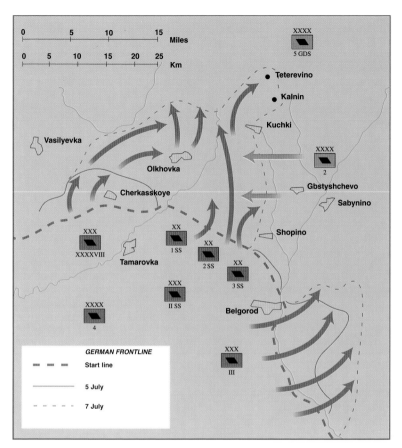

■ *Left:* Waffen-SS and German Army assaults south of Kursk, 4–7 July 1943.

defence line, though. A bridge across the Psel had been blown to prevent a crossing. By mid-afternoon, the Waffen-SS attack had been called off to allow preparations to be made for a more substantial attack the following day. The *Totenkopf* made a night-time raid to seize a key hill above the Psel, but it was driven back. The Soviets kept up their pressure on the right flank of Hausser's corps, sending repeated human-wave attacks against the 167th Infantry Division that had just relieved the *Totenkopf*. Thousands of Russian infantrymen, many of them press-ganged civilians, were mown down by well-aimed artillery fire that was called down within a few hundred metres of the German frontline.

The Soviets were also feeling the strain of battle by this time. Their third line of defence was holding up – but only just. Zhukov had committed all his local reserves. A final decision was now made to commit the strategic reserve. The three tanks corps of the Fifth Guards Tank Army received orders to move westwards to engage the Waffen-SS, and stop them taking a town called Prokhorovka. It would take them three days to be in a position to strike. In the meantime, the troops at the front would have to hold on.

Manstein also realized that the battle was approaching a critical point, and he had prepared orders for XXXXIV Panzer Corps, with the *Wiking* Division in the lead, to start moving towards Belgorod, ready to exploit any breakthrough by Hausser's spearheads. Reports from the northern shoulder of the Kursk salient were not encouraging. The

held out for the morning, trading artillery and mortar fire with the Germans, as well as launching a number of counterattacks. *Totenkopf* commanders led their men forward again in the afternoon, and two bridgeheads were established. It took several hours before bridging equipment could be brought up to allow armour to cross the swollen Psel, to press home the advance. Heavy rain delayed the work, which meant the bridge would not be ready to carry tanks for another day.

## Consolidating the bridgehead

More artillery was brought forward to soften up the Russians to allow the *Totenkopf* to expand its bridgeheads. Stukas joined the assault during the afternoon, and by early evening a third breach had been made in the Soviet defence line. At nightfall three Waffen-SS panzergrenadier battalions were over the Psel, and they held off repeated counterattacks as darkness approached.

On the main road to Prokhorovka, the *Leibstandarte*'s 2nd Panzergrenadier Regiment, reinforced with Tigers, assault guns and Marders, prepared for a dawn attack. Panzers, reconnaissance troops and infantry in armoured halftracks stood ready to exploit the breach. All the division's artillery regiment, backed by rocket launchers and Stukas, pounded the Soviet defence lines on a wooded hill. A battle raged on the slopes and in the woods between Waffen-SS panzergrenadiers and Soviet infantrymen. Soviet artillery joined in the battle, directed from the hills along the northern bank of the Psel. The accurate shell fire brought the *Leibstandarte*'s casualties up to over 200 for the day. Dug-in T-34s had to be destroyed individually by the Tigers, to allow the hill to be taken by the late afternoon. More than 50 Soviet tanks were knocked out and 23 assault guns destroyed. By the time darkness returned to the battlefield, there was still no breakthrough and the panzer kampfgruppe had still to be deployed.

To the south, the *Das Reich* Division was ordered to strike directly eastwards to seize high ground overlooking the main positions of the Waffen-SS corps. The *Deutschland* Panzergrenadier Regiment made some progress at first, but very strong antitank

■ *Above:* **Officers from the army's *Grossdeutschland* Division plan their next move. The division fought on the left flank of II SS Panzer Corps throughout Operation Citadel, suffering heavy casualties.**

German offensive was stalled, and Soviet troops were even starting to drive forward.

Amid heavy summer rain showers, II SS Panzer Corps moved forward again in a coordinated attack to crack open the final line of Russian resistance. The *Totenkopf* Division was now fully deployed to the left of the *Leibstandarte,* and it was launched forward to seize a bridgehead across the Psel. The *Theodor Eicke* Panzergrenadier Regiment led the attack, which was preceded by heavy artillery fire. Assault guns provided close support as the panzergrenadiers stormed the heavily defended villages along the Psel. The Soviet XXXIII Rifle Corps

■ *Left:* Waffen-SS flamethrower teams were used in the first wave of assault operations to neutralize Soviet machine-gun teams and bunkers.

■ *Below:* A Tiger I crew pauses to rest during the height of the offensive.

resistance prevented much progress being made thereafter.

Soviet counterattacks on the Psel bridgehead opened at 08:00 hours on 11 July with a heavy tank attack that was driven off by the *Totenkopf*'s antitank gunners, who knocked out 27 Russian tanks. This allowed work to continue on the bridge, which was capable of carrying the heavy Tiger tanks. Heavy rain and Soviet shelling continued to hamper the work of the Waffen-SS engineers, who did not finish their work until just before midday. The division's 94 tanks then began to cross the river, and plans were put in motion for a major offensive the following day. Victory seemed to be within sight.

> The Leibstandarte *pushed forward again to take the last hill-top pak-front before Prokhorovka*

The *Leibstandarte* pushed forward again to take the last hill-top pak-front before Prokhorovka. Two panzergrenadier battalions led the attack on the hill, which was bristling with antitank guns. They laid down a withering wall of fire which stalled the Waffen-SS attack. Then a wave of T-34s was sent into action against the Germans.

Rocket fire and Stuka support was requested to neutralize the resistance in a barrage that began at 09:00 hours. The air support was directed with great precision by a Luftwaffe forward air controller in an armoured halftrack with the attack troops. The arrival of a detachment of Tiger attacks added to the weight of the assault. Within the hour, the panzergrenadiers had penetrated the Russian trench system and were clearing bunker after bunker. The fighting flowed back and forth as the Russians threw more men into that battle. Stuka raids continued throughout the morning.

Now the *Leibstandarte* panzer kampfgruppe was thrown into the battle, and this turned the tide in the Germans' favour for good. Soviet tank counterattacks against the flanks of the *Leibstandarte* were repulsed. The Russians lost 21 tanks and more than 30 antitank guns. More than 200 Waffen-SS men were killed or wounded during the bitter fighting for the hill. This degenerated into a tank duel along the length of the division's front, involving attacks by small groups of tanks.

## The final Waffen-SS assault

Satisfied with their success over the Psel and in front of Prokhorovka, Hausser's staff now set about planning the following day's drive to complete the piercing of the Soviet third defence line. More artillery was to be brought up to blast the Russians out of their bunkers on the hill above the *Totenkopf's* bridgehead. Once this was complete, the *Leibstandarte* and *Das Reich* Divisions would surge forward to seize Prokhorovka. With the resistance destroyed, the panzers were to be unleashed into the open country beyond.

The Waffen-SS panzer regiments were rested during the night to prepare them for the coming major attack. Repair teams worked to ensure the maximum number of panzers were available. During the evening the *Leibstandarte* mustered five Panzer IIIs, 47 Panzer IVs and four Tiger Is ready for action; *Das Reich* fielded 34 Panzer IIIs, 18 Panzer IVs, one Tiger I and eight captured T-34s; and the *Totenkopf* had operational 54 Panzer IIIs, 30 Panzer IVs and 10 Tiger Is. II SS Panzer Corps was also able to field 60 StuG IIIs and a similar number of Marder self-propelled antitank guns. In total, Hausser would have more than 300 armoured vehicles available for action.

He and his staff were convinced they were only a few hours away from achieving the decisive breakthrough and ultimate victory on the Eastern Front. They had no idea that only a few kilometres from the *Leibstandarte's* advance posts, a force of more than 800 tanks and assault guns were massing to strike at them the following morning.

Marshal Pavel Rotmistrov had just led his Fifth Guards Tank Army on a 320km (200-mile) road march to Prokhorovka, and had spent the day preparing to launch it into action. He brought with him the fresh XVIII and XXIX Tank Corps and the Fifth Guards Mechanized Corps. To bolster his attack wave, he was assigned II Tank Corps or II Guards Tank Corps, which had already been blooded in the past week's clashes with the Waffen-SS. This force included 500 T-34s, with the remainder being light T-70s or lend-lease British Churchill and American General Lee tanks. Rotmistrov was Stalin's most experienced tank commander, and he set about preparing his mammoth tank force

■ *Below:* Waffen-SS panzergrenadiers endured the stress of battle around the clock during the offensive, attacking again and again in the face of overwhelming odds.

■ *Above:* Waffen-SS Panzer IIIs move across the steppe in attack formation. The tanks at the rear are hanging back, ready to manoeuvre to engage the flanks of any Russian antitank batteries that engage the first wave of panzers.

for action with great professionalism. The road march was accomplished in conditions of great secrecy under heavy fighter cover, and when his tanks halted to rest and refuel they were hidden in forest assembly areas. They gathered in the gullies and forests to the east and north of Prokhorovka under the cover of darkness, and awaited their orders.

Their commander recognized that, tank crew for tank crew, his men were no match for their German opponents. Only a few months before many had been factory workers who had built their tanks and then driven them to the front. Rotmistrov realized that once under way, his force would soon run out of control. Most Soviet tanks did not have radios, and commanders controlled their subordinates by means of coloured flags. Rotmistrov gave his corps and brigade commanders simple orders, little more than specific objectives and axes of advance. The main way he could influence the battle was by tightly controlling the timing of when he

committed his tank brigades, so the Soviet marshal set up his forward command post on a hill southwest of Prokhorovka, from where he could see all the key terrain and get a "finger tip" feel for the course of the battle. The Soviet marshal spent most of the night making final preparations for the mass attack, which was to start just after 06:00 hours the following morning, 12 July.

The Battle of Prokhorovka effectively took place in an area little more than 8km by 8km (five miles by five miles) – it was smaller than the battlefield at Waterloo. The terrain where the main engagement of the battle was to unfold was flat and rolling. The main Waffen-SS tank forces were concentrated on a hill 1.6km (one mile) southwest of Prokhorovka. The ground gently slopped down towards the town, but then a small ridge line created an area of dead ground, behind which Rotmistrov had concentrated his main tank strike forces – XVIII and XXIX Tank Corps. A railway line and embankment, running southwest from Prokhorovka, created a natural division of the battlefield, meaning the Russians had to employ two distinct axes of attack. The railway line also formed the divisional boundary between the *Leibstandarte*, north of it, and *Das Reich*, to its south.

To the northwest of this gladiatorial arena was the River Psel, and the high ground on the northern bank of the river dominated the assembly area of the main Waffen-SS assault force – the *Leibstandarte* Division. The high ground was far too distant for direct tank fire from it to be a threat, but it provided a superb artillery observation vantage point. Whoever controlled this high ground dominated the battlefield. The valley along the Psel, with its small woods and villages, also provided a covered approach route to infiltrate behind the high ground above Prokhorovka.

> *Above the Psel, infantry battalions of the Soviet XXXI Tank Corps kicked off the Russian offensive*

Running south from Prokhorovka was a series of forested hills, running in a north-south direction, which were intersected by deep gullies and streams, making them poor ground for tanks.

Above the Psel, infantry battalions of the Soviet XXXI Tank Corps, without tank support, kicked off the Russian offensive by attacking during the night. The *Totenkopf* Division saw off the attack after hand-to-hand fighting in the villages around its bridgehead. In the face of heavy Soviet artillery, air raids and Stalin's Organ rocket fire, the *Totenkopf* Division's panzergrenadiers began their attack as scheduled just after dawn. The division's panzer regiment was now over the River Psel, and was poised to strike out once a route through the Soviet defences became apparent. Elements of the *Totenkopf*'s panzer kampfgruppe were committed at 07:15

■ *Below:*
*Totenkopf* Panzer IIIs carrying panzergrenadiers watch an artillery barrage pummelling Soviet defensive positions. The Swastika flag is an air recognition sign to prevent the Luftwaffe mistaking the Waffen-SS tanks for Soviet vehicles.

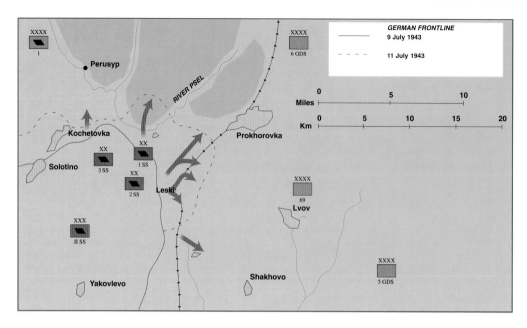

| GERMAN FRONTLINE | |
| --- | --- |
| ———— | 9 July 1943 |
| - - - - | 11 July 1943 |

hours, and they helped punch a first hole in the Soviet line.

All during the night, the forward outposts of the *Leibstandarte* were sending back reports to their headquarters, saying they were hearing noise from large numbers of tanks. In places Soviets tanks tried to probe the German line and, as dawn broke, scores of Russian fighter-bombers attacked the division's frontline positions, artillery fire bases and supply columns. It was becoming clear that something was wrong, but the Germans had no idea what it was. The division's panzer kampfgruppe was ordered to proceed with its early morning attack directly towards Prokhorovka, with the Tiger tank company in the lead. The *Das Reich's* *Deutschland* Panzergrenadier Regiment was lined up as well, ready to advance northwards on the south side of the *Leibstandarte*.

Almost like clockwork, at 06:30 hours both the *Leibstandarte's* panzers and the Soviet XXIX Tank Corps were waved forward by their commanders. In the morning haze, the Waffen-SS panzer crews spotted a mass of tanks 4.8–6.4km (3–4 miles) directly in front of them, on the far side of the valley. Some 60 tanks – a whole brigade of XXIX Tank Corps – were heading straight

for them. Artillery fire and Katyusha rockets started to land among the German tanks. At the extreme limit of their range – 2000m (6562ft) – the 50 or so Waffen-SS tanks started to pick-off the Soviet tanks. Rotmistrov had briefed his tank commanders not to stop to trade fire with the Germans, but to charge at full speed to make it more difficult to be hit, and to allow them to get into a position to hit the enemy tanks at close quarters on their more vulnerable side armour. The charge of the T-34s was a death ride. The Russian crews followed their orders to the letter, but by 09:00 hours the steppe was littered with burning hulks. The *Leibstandarte* tank crews had destroyed their enemy for almost no loss thanks to their long-range gunnery skills.

Rotmistrov's first wave also hit the *Das Reich* Division, with a brigade of XXIX Tank Corps taking a pounding from the *Leibstandarte's* artillery as it moved forward. Then the *Das Reich* panzers put down withering fire to halt their attack. Rotmistrov now started to launch his brigades forward on an hourly basis in an attempt to batter through the German lines.

Next on the receiving end of an attack from XVIII Tank Corps was the *Totenkopf's*

*Theodor Eicke* Panzergrenadier Regiment in the Psel valley. Two Soviet infantry regiments backed by 50 tanks, pushed forward into the *Totenkopf*'s right flank at 07.:45 hours, to be seen off by the division's assault gun battalion.

At almost the same time, artillery and rocket fire rained down on the *Leibstandarte*'s 1st Panzergrenadier Regiment, which was holding the ground to the right of the division's panzer kampfgruppe. After an hour of softening-up artillery fire, the Russian armour was sent into action. The defenders were given a warning from a Luftwaffe reconnaissance patrol that a tank brigade was approaching along the railway line. Some 40 T-34s of XXIX Tank Corps were then among the German trenches. More were following behind in a second wave, along with hordes of Red infantry. Waffen-SS tank-hunting teams went to work taking on the

Russian vehicles, but it took the intervention of five Marder self-propelled guns to see off the tanks.

Farther to the east, the *Leibstandarte*'s panzers were now attacked from two directions by more than 70 tanks of XVIII Tank Corps. An advance guard of seven panzers was overrun in the charge, losing four tanks to point-blank fire as the T-34s surged past them. The remaining three panzers were ignored by the Russian tanks, who were now heading directly for the main panzer kampfgruppe. The "lost" panzers turned to follow the T-34s, picking off 20 of them before the main panzer line opened fire with a mass volley. Stunned by the sudden burst of fire, the Russians halted to trade fire with the Germans. The 33 tanks of the panzer kampfgruppe now counterattacked, moving into flanking positions and raking the mass of confused Russian tanks with gunfire. After three hours of swirling

> ### Farther to the east, the Leibstandarte's panzers were now attacked from two directions

■ *Below:* The *Das Reich* Division's Tiger I tanks spearheaded the unit's attacks at the height of the battles around Prokhorovka.

action, the Germans claimed to have knocked out 62 T-70s and T-34s.

The *Totenkopf* Division continued to be pressed by XVIII Tank Corps, which committed its 32nd Motorized Infantry Brigade at 10:00 hours to another battle in the Psel valley. Some 50 tanks, including T-34s, T-70s and Churchills, were again driven off by the *Totenkopf*, which claimed 20 kills. At almost hourly intervals, Soviet infantry attacks were launched against all sides of the *Totenkopf*'s bridgehead to keep the pressure on the German left flank. Harassing artillery fire was also regularly directed at the two tank bridges to try to prevent reinforcements moving into the bridgehead.

The *Leibstandarte*'s commander, Theodor Wisch, was forward monitoring the battle from a hill just behind the panzer kampfgruppe. He watched as a group of T-34s managed to break free from the battle with the *Totenkopf* and swing right into the *Leibstandarte*'s flank held by its reconnaissance unit. A handful of Russian tanks managed to get past the reconnaissance battalion's antitank guns, and charged forward into the division's rear area, shooting up

trucks and small groups of Waffen-SS men until they were put out of action by the *Leibstandarte*'s artillery regiment firing its guns in the antitank mode.

By early afternoon the battle in front of Prokhorovka reached its climax, first with Russian infantry supported by tanks advancing directly out of the town towards the *Leibstandarte*'s panzergrenadiers. A panzer counterattack broke up the infantry formation, and 40 tanks were claimed destroyed at long range. An hour later, the panzer kampfgruppe was moved northeastwards to clear out the 100 or so Soviet tanks believed to be hiding in the Psel valley. The *Leibstandarte*'s three remaining Tigers were then placed at the front of the panzerkeil. The force had only moved a few hundred metres when directly ahead more than 100 T-34s could be seen charging towards the German formation. This was the last hurrah of Rotmistrov's XVIII Tank Corps, and would see the destruction of the whole of the 181st Tank Brigade.

At a range of 1800m (5905ft), the Tigers started to take a toll of the Russian tanks. One after another the T-34s exploded in

■ *Above: Totenkopf* **panzergrenadiers march forward to occupy positions in the Psel valley as the division pushes forward to outflank the Soviet defences at Prokhorovka.**

huge fireballs. Still the Russians kept coming. At 1000m (3280ft), every shot from the Tigers' 88mm cannons were scoring hits. Up to 10 tanks a minute were being hit as the Soviet brigade continued to surge forward. The Russians tried to return fire, but they were firing on the move, and few of them were able to hit any of the German tanks. Now the famous incident occurred when a T-34 tried to ram the Tiger of the famous *Leibstandarte* tank commander, SS-Untersturmführer Michael Wittmann, at high speed. The Tiger survived the impact and was able to back-off from the wrecked Russian tank before its ammunition exploded. The 181st Tank Brigade failed to penetrate the German line, and for much of the afternoon the *Leibstandarte*'s panzers hunted down its remnants along the northern edge of the battlefield.

A tank brigade tried to launch an attack from the Psel valley later in the afternoon, but its T-34s barely got forward from their assembly area before accurate German 88mm fire from the Tigers broke up the attack. In the Psel valley the remnants of several Soviet tank brigades and battalions were trying to sort themselves out after being rebuffed with heavy losses during the day's battles. Commanders were trying to muster scratch battalions from the survivors, in order to rejoin the fight. Two more attacks were attempted

*Up to 10 tanks a minute were being hit as the Soviet brigade continued to surge forward*

■ *Below: Das Reich* Division Tiger Is regroup during the final phase of the battles to the south of Prokhorovka.

towards the end of the afternoon, only to get the same reception from the German tanks. The Soviet tank crews were now starting to show a healthy respect for the Waffen-SS panzers, and made few attempts to emerge from cover. In addition, the *Leibstandarte* Division's artillery regiment now started to direct regular barrages into the area to make sure that the Russian troops kept their heads down.

On the *Das Reich*'s front the battle was equally fierce, with two tank corps and several infantry divisions trying to batter through its position from late in the morning. The brunt of these attacks were borne by the division's two panzergrenadier regiments, *Der Führer* in the south and *Deutschland* to the immediate right of *Leibstandarte*, which set up a series of defensive fronts in the woods and gullies south of Prokhorovka. II Tank and II Guards Tank Corps had already been blooded against the Waffen-SS over the previous week, and were now far more cautious in exposing their tanks to German firepower.

A series of coordinated brigade-sized infantry and armour attacks were launched throughout the day, beginning at 11:40 hours with a push against *Der Führer*'s sec-

ond battalion led by 30 T-34s. At the same time, an infantry attack hit *Deutschland*'s front.

Barely had the *Das Reich* Division seen off these human-wave infantry assaults, when *Der Führer* was bounced by a two-pronged attack. The regiment's front was engulfed by thousands of Russian infantry charging forward at the Waffen-SS lines. One German battalion also counted 40 Russian tanks advancing towards its lines among the infantry. In the north of the regiment's sector, another 70 tanks tried to push through to the Belgorod–Prokhorovka railway line at 14:00 hours.

Waffen-SS assault guns and antitank guns were pushed forward to repulse the Russian attacks, which went on well into the afternoon. At 15:00 hours, *Das Reich*'s panzer kampfgruppe was mustered from its reserve positions to counterattack and neutralize the Soviet threat once and for all. Two Soviet tank brigades were decimated in the sweep and 21 T-34s destroyed. This calmed the situation for a few hours. The Soviets were not finished yet, though, and they pushed forward again at 17:00 hours to try to force a breach between *Das Reich* and the 167th Infantry Division. As nightfall

■ *Below:* A Waffen-SS 20mm flak gun team tries to get the attention of Luftwaffe aircraft operating over the Kursk battle area, to prevent an accidental attack on friendly forces.

approached, the Soviet attack on *Das Reich* had well and truly run out steam.

Over on the western flank of the battlefield, the *Totenkopf* Division was still battling to break out of its bridgehead. As the pressure mounted on German defences in front of Prokhorovka during the morning, the division was ordered to swing a kampfgruppe back across the Psel to strike into the Soviet armour using the valley as a base to attack the *Leibstandarte* Division. This attack made some progress and kept the Soviets bottled up in their "valley of death" for the rest of the day. The schwerpunkt of the division's efforts was to the north, and at 12:30 hours its panzer kampfgruppe was launched northwards through a huge barrage of Katyusha rocket fire. The *Totenkopf's* panzers, with their 10 Tiger tanks in the lead, swept all before them. Its advance rolled 3.2km (two miles) north to

*This attack made some progress and kept the Soviets bottled up in their "valley of death"*

cut the main road north out of Prokhorovka, and only the onset of darkness brought it to a halt. The division's panzers claimed the destruction of 27 Russian tanks in the advance. Follow-up panzergrenadiers made slower progress in the face of determined Soviet infantry, who fought to the last in the villages and woods around the bridgehead. This meant only a narrow corridor could be kept open from the bridgehead to the panzer spearhead to the north. Soviet counterattacks and artillery barrages rained down on the *Totenkopf* Division well into the night, inflicting heavy casualties. The division's panzers suffered heavily, with more than 45 out of 94 being put out of action, including all of its Tigers. Heavy rain showers washed the battlefield during the early evening, extinguishing many of the 400 burning tank hulks that were arrayed in

■ *Above:* Waffen-SS panzer-grenadiers move through a burning Russian village. Hand grenades and MG 42 machine guns were their weapons of choice for close-quarter combat with Soviet infantry.

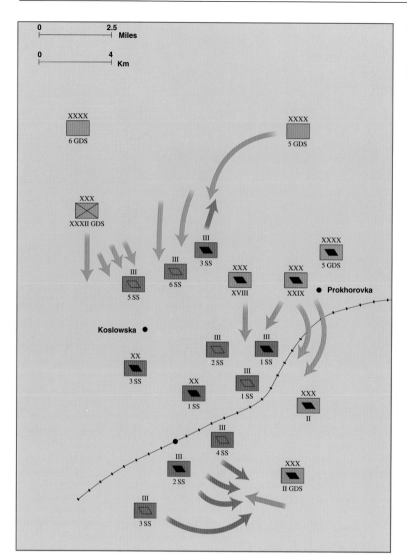

■ *Left:*
**Prokhorovka on 12
July 1943 – the
high watermark of
Operation Citadel.**

front of the German lines. In the rain, repair crews from both sides tried to recover the remains of the damaged tanks to patch them up for next day's combat.

A string of top Soviet generals visited the battlefield to congratulate Rotmistrov on his great "victory". He had stopped the élite of Hitler's hated SS in their tracks and still held Prokhorovka. When Rotmistrov toured his shattered command to see for himself if it could be made ready for action the follow-

ing day, he could be forgiven for thinking he had suffered a massive defeat. XXIX Tank Corps had lost 60 percent of its tanks and XVIII Tank Corps had suffered 30 percent losses. On 13 July, Rotmistrov admitted that his tank army could only field 100 to 150 combat-ready tanks out of the 850 committed for action at Prokhorovka on the previous day. The remainder had been destroyed or were too badly damaged to be considered fit for action.

Controversy has surrounded German tank losses in this crucial battle, with Rotmistrov and other Soviet histories claiming the Waffen-SS lost more than 300 tanks, including 70 Tiger tanks, during the action in front of Prokhorovka during 12 July. German records, however, paint a different picture. The Germans admitted to losing 70 to 80 tanks on that day, the majority of which were lost by the *Totenkopf* Division. The *Das Reich*'s mechanics had already repaired scores of tanks damaged earlier in the offensive, so that on the morning of 13 July they actually had more tanks available than on the day before; while the *Leibstandarte* Division was only some 17 tanks down on the previous day's total.

When Hausser saw the tank kill claims coming from the battlefield, he could scarcely believe his eyes. The *Leibstandarte* Division alone claimed 192 Soviet tanks destroyed. The Waffen-SS general thought this was scarcely credible until he visited the battlefield and walked around the hulks, numbering them with chalk to confirm the kills. Rotmistrov's own admissions of his tank losses tally in many ways with German figures, indicating that his tank charge, when considered on its own, might be classed as one of the most disastrous actions in military history.

After a night of rest, the battle resumed with a desultory infantry battle along the whole of the battle front. The Russians now started to push their infantry forward in major attacks, backed by heavy artillery fire, to compensate for their enormous tank losses. The *Leibstandarte*'s panzers and reconnaissance troops pushed forward to probe the strength of the Russian defences. Heavy antitank fire met the German patrols, and they withdrew back to their lines.

The *Totenkopf* Division was the main target of the Soviet effort. The division's understrength panzer kampfgruppe acted as a fire brigade inside the Psel bridgehead, moving to threatened sectors to stamp out Russian breakthroughs. The Red Air Force was now making its presence felt over the battlefield in strength, and the *Totenkopf*'s flak gunners were much in demand to protect the division from Stormovik fighter-bombers. Soviet tank losses continued to mount along the Psel front, with 38 T-34s alone being destroyed by the *Totenkopf*'s antitank battalion during one 20-minute incursion.

The offensive strength of II Waffen-SS Panzer Corps now rested in the *Das Reich* Division, and it pushed forward to attempt to link up with III Panzer Corps that was pushing northwards from east of Belgorod. *Das Reich*'s Tiger company spearheaded the advance that brushed aside several Russian tank counterattacks on 13 and 14 July, destroying at least eight T-34s. The advance continued for two more days, with village after village having to be cleared of Soviet defenders. On the morning of 15 July, it linked up with the 7th Panzer Division to close the ring around several thousand Red Army soldiers of XXXXVIII Rifle Corps and II Guards Tank Corps. An attempt to push northwards to outflank Prokhorovka from the east ran into heavy defences. As the *Das Reich* battled forward, the *Leibstandarte* and *Totenkopf* Divisions set about rebuilding their strength for another push northwards to finish off the Fifth Guards Tank Army for good. They were not to get the opportunity.

On 13 July, Hitler summoned his Eastern Front commanders to his East Prussian headquarters to issue new orders. Three days before, British and American troops had landed in Sicily, and the Ninth Army on the northern shoulder of the Kursk salient had been hit by a massive Soviet offensive that sent it reeling backwards in confusion. Hitler wanted to strip the Eastern Front of troops to shore up the Mediterranean.

Manstein pleaded to be allowed to continue his offensive to smash the last Soviet armoured reserves along the southern shoulder of the salient. Hitler agreed to this limited objective, but his attention was now focused on ensuring that the Italians were

*The division's panzer kampfgruppe acted as a fire brigade inside the Psel bridgehead*

not knocked out of the war by further allied moves in the Mediterranean. XXIV Panzer Corps was not to be committed to exploit any success that II SS Panzer Corps might achieve. The final nails in the coffin of Operation Citadel were new Soviet offensives on 17 July, far to the south along the River Mius Front and at Izyum, which threatened the German hold on the strategically important southern Ukraine. These operations were deliberate deception, or maskirovka, moves, timed to distract German armour from the Kursk Front, which was entering a critical phase with Soviet tank reserves all but exhausted. Hitler fell for the ruse, ordering that II SS Panzer Corps be pulled out of the battle for the Kursk salient and sent southwards to neutralize this new threat. Operation Citadel was officially over.

The *Totenkopf*'s bridgehead over the Psel represented the high watermark of the Third Reich. Manstein and former Waffen-SS generals later claimed that if the Führer had held his nerve for a few more days, victory would have been achieved. The Waffen-SS claimed a huge number of tank kills – 1149 in total – during Operation Citadel, along with the destruction of 459 antitank guns, 85 aircraft and 47 artillery pieces. Hausser's men also took 6441 prisoners. This, indeed, could be considered a great tactical victory. However, from the Soviet viewpoint the battle was a strategic success. Their defence tactics worked, preventing the Germans breaking through into the open and using their Blitzkrieg-style of warfare to outflank, confuse and surround the Russians. The cost in lives and tanks was huge, but the Germans were never able to create a decisive breakthrough. Hitler would not give his commanders the time they needed to punch through to Kursk.

Fires were breaking out all along the borders of the Third Reich. Hitler insisted on rushing Waffen-SS panzer divisions to wherever a crisis loomed. They had become the Führer's "Fire Brigade". The Soviet High Command, however, fully understood Germany's many weaknesses and devised a strategy to defeat them. They held out at Prokhorovka – only just – and immediately applied pressure elsewhere to force the Germans to pull out their steadily dwindling panzer divisions to plug the holes. The Waffen-SS panzers may have been masters of the battlefield at Prokhorovka, but the Soviets were now masters of strategy on the Eastern Front. From now on the Wehrmacht would dance to the Red Army's tune.

The carefully gathered panzer reserves had been largely spent, while the Red Army, though perhaps suffering up to 250,000 casualties at Kursk, was now free to launch its own strategic offensive on the Eastern Front. As Manstein stated: "Henceforth

*The Waffen-SS claimed a huge number of tank kills – 1149 in total – during Operation Citadel*

Southern Army Group found itself waging a defensive struggle which could not be anything more than a system of improvisations and stop-gaps. Being too weak, on that widely extended front, for purely passive defence against an enemy so many times stronger than itself, it had to concentrate its efforts – even at the risk of repercussions in sectors temporarily less threatened – on punctually assembling forces whenever there was a Soviet breakthrough to intercept or a chance of inflicting a blow on the enemy. What had to be avoided at all costs was that any elements of the Army Group should become cut off through deep enemy breakthroughs and suffer the same fate as Sixth Army at Stalingrad. To 'maintain ourselves in the field', and in doing so wear down the enemy's offensive capacity to the utmost, became the whole essence of this struggle."

And during the final period of the war on the Eastern Front, up to the very end of the Third Reich, the Waffen-SS panzer divisions would be called upon again and again by a desperate Führer to save seemingly impossible situations.

■ *Below:* The Soviet Fifth Guards Tank Army paid a heavy price during the Battle at Prokhorovka, losing more than 400 tanks.

# CHAPTER 3

# KESSEL BATTLES

## The Cherkassy and Kamenets Podolsk Pockets.

**K**essel is the German word for kettle. It is also the German military term for a "battle of encirclement". The analogy is appropriate. Once caught in a pocket by enemy pincers, any trapped troops are put under increasing pressure until a boiling point is reached. In the face of dwindling supplies, the trapped troops would either have to break out or face destruction.

Weakened by a steady stream of losses since the Battle of Kursk in July 1943, the Wehrmacht's Eastern Front was in tatters by January 1944. It was held by a rag-tag collection of divisions that were lucky to each be able to put 5000 fit soldiers into their front-line trenches. As for mobile reserves, they were also all but exhausted. Even the élite panzer divisions of the Waffen-SS were lucky if they could scrape together 30 battered and worn-out tanks that could be defined as "combat ready". It was only a matter of time before the Soviet High Command exploited this weakness, and started to chop up the German Army Group South into small chunks and annihilate them. Field Marshal Erich von Manstein had a reputation for being Germany's master strategist, but by January 1944 even he was running out of tricks to "magic" his battered frontline back together again.

The Soviet breakthrough southwest of Kiev during December 1943 pushed the German Fourth Panzer Army back over 160km

■ *Left:* The Ukraine in February 1944. A Waffen-SS Tiger I tank moves across a bleak, desolate winter landscape towards a desperate battle against overwhelming odds.

(100 miles), leaving the Eighth Army's right flank dangerously exposed. In January 1944, it was the only German formation with a foothold on the southern banks of the River Dnieper. True to form, Hitler refused to let it withdraw to safety, and it was therefore only a matter of time before the Soviet High Command closed the net around it. The core of the Eighth Army's defence was the Waffen-SS *Wiking* Panzergrenadier Division. Usually, it had only a dozen Panzer IIIs, eight Panzer IVs and four Sturmgeschütz (StuG) IIIs ready for action on any day during January 1944. The division also boasted the Walloon Assault Brigade made up of Nazi Flemish volunteers from northern Belgium.

## More than 600 Russian tanks opened a huge breach in the German line and trapped four divisions

The Soviets made their first attempt to surround the Eighth Army in early January, with another steamroller offensive aimed at smashing XLVII Panzer Corps deployed to defend Kirovograd, which protected the route to the German rear. More than 600 Russian tanks opened a huge breach in the German line and trapped four German divisions in the sprawling industrial city. "Kirovograd sounds too much like Stalingrad for my liking", was the comment of the garrison commander, who took advantage of a breakdown in radio communications with higher command to order his troops to march to freedom. They successfully broke out with all their tanks and heavy artillery. The line

■ *Above:* A column of *Leibstandarte* Division reconnaissance troops pause before heading into action again. Their unique mix of vehicles and weapons gave them great mobility and hitting power.

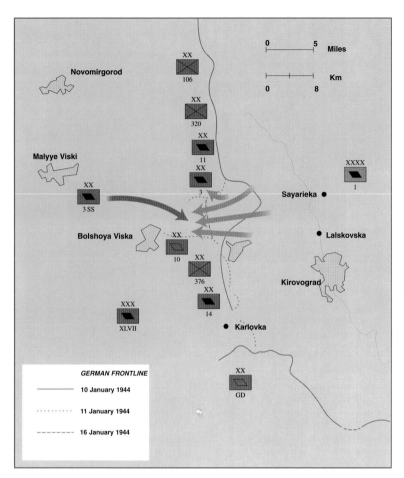

Novomirgorod

XX
106

XX
320

XX
11

Malyye Viski

XX
3

XXXX
1

Sayarieka ●

XX
3 SS

Bolshoya Viska

XX
10

Lalskovska ●

XX
376

Kirovograd

XXX
XLVII

XX
14

Karlovka ●

**GERMAN FRONTLINE**

──────── 10 January 1944

·············· 11 January 1944

- - - - - - - 16 January 1944

XX
GD

■ *Left:* The *Totenkopf* Division stabilizes the front near Kirovograd, 10–16 January 1944.

was rebuilt after Manstein moved in two fresh divisions to mount a counterattack. Leading this effort was the Waffen-SS *Totenkopf* Division, which had been brought up from the lower Dnieper. Just as the Soviets were preparing for a final push, the *Totenkopf* burst upon them and scattered several Russian divisions. This was only a temporary respite, though.

Manstein now tried to turn the tables on the Soviet First Tank Army that was pushing southwards into the Eighth Army's exposed left flank. He pulled together a scratch force of three "divisions", under army panzer General Hermann Breith, and launched them eastwards into the flank of the Russian tank force. Heavy mud delayed the deploy-

ment of the *Leibstandarte* Division into position to lead Breith's III Panzer Corps. Backed by fire from the Wehrmacht's only artillery division, the Waffen-SS troops sliced into the flank of the Soviet spearhead. Heavy mud made the going heavy, but with its Tigers in the lead the division swept all before it. By 28 January it had closed the ring around several Russian divisions. The Germans claimed 8000 Russians dead, 701 tanks destroyed and 5436 prisoners.

This success was occurring at the same time as another Soviet advance was moving to trap the German Eighth Army on 24 January. Two armoured pincers sliced into the thinly held flanks of the army and met up on 28 January to close the noose around

56,000 men of the German XI and XLII
Corps, forming what has since become
known as either the Korsun or Cherkassy
Pocket. The only German armoured unit in
the pocket was the *Wiking* Division.

Just as at Stalingrad, Hitler ordered the
troops in the pocket to stand firm and wait
for a rescue force to restore the front behind
them. In the meantime, an air bridge would
keep them supplied with food, fuel and
ammunition. It was a fantasy. Soviet fighters
started to take a
huge toll on the
Luftwaffe supply
aircraft. On the
ground, more than
500 Soviet tanks
were ringing the
pocket, and Man-
stein could only muster four worn-out panzer divisions to mount a rescue mission.
Hitler would give him no fresh troops from
Western Europe because of the Anglo-
American threat to France. Breith, meanwhile, was ordered to complete his opera-

tion against the encircled Russian force to
the west and then batter his way through to
the Eighth Army.

The army's 16th and 17th Panzer
Divisions spearheaded the break-in operation, with the composite "Bake" Heavy
Panzer Regiment in the lead. This unit was
at this time the most powerful German tank
unit on the Eastern Front, boasting 47
Panther and 34 Tiger I tanks, supported by
armoured infantry and self-propelled units.

Attacking north-
wards on 4 February
in an attempt to
turn the tables on
the Soviet tank force
and trap it in a
pocket, the rescue
force at first made
good progress across frozen ground. A sudden thaw now turned the battlefield into a
quagmire. III Panzer Corps' advance literally got bogged down. Wheeled fuel tankers
and ammunition trucks just could not
move. Even tracked vehicles had difficulties.

> *Just as at Stalingrad, Hitler
> ordered the troops in the
> pocket to stand firm and
> wait for a rescue force*

■ *Right:* Panzer IVs loaded with panzergrenadiers disappear into the winter gloom in another attempt to batter through to the 56,000 troops trapped in the Cherkassy Pocket.

■ *Below:* German antitank defences in the Ukraine were bolstered by scores of Nashorn self-propelled guns, fitted with versions of the 88mm gun.

At times fuel for the tanks even had to be carried forward to the front in buckets or cans. The *Leibstandarte* Division battled on for 32km (20 miles). Its Tiger company destroyed 26 Soviet tanks as it established a bridgehead over the River Gniloy Tikich on 8 February 1944.

With its northward advance stalled, III Panzer Corps now moved the *Leibstandarte* Division and the army's 1st Panzer Division southwards so they could attack directly eastwards towards the pocket. This switch confused the Soviets, and the advance moved forward again, with the Waffen-SS on the left and the 1st Panzer on right. Again frost helped the tank advance, and the 1st Panzer Division was able to throw a bridgehead over the Gniloy Tikich at Lyssinka, only 8km (five miles) from the trapped troops. A huge pak-front of 52 anti-tank guns and 80 T-34s barred its way, though. The 16th Panzer Division and the Bake Regiment tried to outflank the enemy defences by pushing north, but they were soon stopped by heavy enemy fire.

As the *Leibstandarte* Division tried to keep up with the advance, it was hit by huge Soviet tank attacks. First V Rifle Corps, followed by XVI Tank Corps, surged forward. It was all the understrength Waffen-SS division could do to hold off the nonstop attacks that swept forward out of the thick forests. The division's Tiger company was at the centre of the defence, knocking out scores of Russian tanks as they streamed forward.

The battle went on for days. Soviet tanks washed around the small German units holding open the 1.6km- (one-mile-) wide corridor eastwards. Several times the Russians cut the corridor, and counterattacks had to be mounted to clear out their infantry and tanks. By 16 February, the 1st Panzer Division, helped by *Leibstandarte*

*Several times the Russians cut the corridor, and counterattacks had to be mounted*

■ *Above:* The breakout from the Cherkassy Pocket through the Lyssinka bridgehead, 11–20 February 1944.

panzergrenadiers, was holding on to its bridgehead by its fingernails. Only 60 men and a dozen Panther tanks were across the river, holding off daily attacks by V Guards Tanks Corps. III Panzer Corps just did not have enough strength to mount the final push to open a corridor to the trapped troops. During the afternoon, Manstein ordered XI and XLII Corps to break out west that evening. He avoided consulting the Führer's headquarters to prevent his orders being countermanded.

Inside the pocket, artillery General Wilhelm Stemmermann was not going to repeat the mistakes of Field Marshal Freidrich Paulus at Stalingrad, and he immediately prepared to follow Manstein's orders. There was no time to lose.

The trapped troops were organized into three assault columns and a rearguard for the break-out. *Wiking* formed the southern column. Its last remaining Panzer IIIs and StuG IIIs led the advance, which began at 23:00 hours on 16 February. The first assault went in silently, with German infantry bayoneting Soviet sentries. This established paths through the Soviet inner ring, and then the *Wiking*'s tanks fanned out to provide flank protection for the ragged column.

*As usual, the Russians massed huge breakthrough forces close to their chosen pressure points*

The other two columns, made up of two infantry divisions, used guile to slip through the Russian lines to link up with 1st Panzer Division. *Wiking*'s column soon ran into trouble when a storm of Russian machine-gun and tank fire started to rake it. SS-Obergruppenführer Herbert Gille, *Wiking*'s commander, ordered one of his battalions to deal with this threat, while the rest of his division skirted around to the south of the Russian blocking position. When the Waffen-SS grenadiers reached the Gniloy Tikich, they abandoned all their heavy equipment and swam the freezing river before finding safety.

It was then the rearguard's turn to move out, and soon the two infantry divisions were being bombarded from the blocking position that had hampered *Wiking*'s escape attempt. They too broke and ran for the Gniloy Tikich. The few kilometres to the river were soon littered with abandoned trucks, cars, wagons, artillery pieces and tanks, as well as the bodies of 15,000 dead Germans. Among them was their commander, Stemmermann, who died when a tank shell ripped into the wagon he was travelling in.

Throughout the night and into the morning, the pathetic survivors of the pocket staggered past the men of the 1st Panzer and *Leibstandarte* Divisions. The hardened panzer troops were shocked at the poor morale of the survivors. They started to talk about "Kessel shock" – a penetrating fear of capture by the Soviets that overrode normal discipline and led to the breakdown of unit cohesion in time of crisis.

The 1st Panzer Division held its bridgehead open for two more days, though only some 30,000 men found their way to German lines. The *Wiking* Division was shattered, and was now reduced to less than half of its established strength. Only 600 troops out of the Walloon Brigade's 2000 men escaped.

The survivors were soon shipped away from the front, and III Panzer Corps pulled back to establish a defence line ready to repel the inevitable next Soviet offensive. During late February Manstein reorganized his remaining panzer divisions as best he could, but there was now a feeling that the next Soviet onslaught would be unstoppable, wherever it struck.

Stalin now sent his strategic genius, Marshal Georgi Zhukov, to supervise the final destruction of Manstein's army group. He was to personally lead a pincer attack into the left wing of Manstein's front, and another attack on the other flank would eventually seal the trap around the First and Fourth Panzer Armies. If the attack succeeded, 200,000 Germans would be cut off and destroyed in the biggest Kessel battle since Stalingrad.

As usual, the Russians massed huge breakthrough forces close to their chosen pressure points. Whole divisions of artillery

**■ Above:** Large numbers of Panther tanks saw service with the *Leibstandarte* Division in the Ukraine, inflicting heavy losses on the Soviets.

blasted the German lines for days, and then several hundred T-34s were launched forward to drive over the ruins. The targets were two weak infantry corps, which soon folded when the Soviet attacks went in on 4 and 5 March 1944. In a matter of days Zhukov's tank corps covered more than 160km (100 miles), and most of Manstein's army group – 22 divisions – found itself cut off in a huge Kessel or pocket centred around the town of Kamenets Podolsk. The cut-off troops included the cream of the Wehrmacht's panzer divisions, as well as both the *Leibstandarte* and *Das Reich* Waffen-SS Divisions. Command of the trapped troops fell to the First Panzer Army's commander, Colonel-General Hans Hube. The one-armed tank commander had actually served under Paulus at Stalingrad, and he would soon put into practice some of the lessons he had learned in that Kessel battle.

> *Command of the trapped troops fell to the First Panzer Army's commander, Colonel-General Hans Hube*

Just before Stalingrad fell, Hitler ordered Hube to be evacuated because he had earmarked him for rapid promotion.

Still serving with III Panzer Corps, the *Leibstandarte* Division was in the path of Zhukov's massive southward pincer. With only a dozen operational Panthers and a handful of other tanks and assault guns to hand, the division had no hope of stopping the several hundred Russian tanks that streamed through the breach in the Eastern Front. The Waffen-SS played an instrumental part in rescuing several army infantry divisions that looked as if they might be overrun. At this point it became the cornerstone of the west-facing front of the pocket. Over on the eastern edge of the pocket, the *Das Reich* kampfgruppe was in an equally precarious position, with six Panthers, five Panzer IVs and four StuG IIIs ready for action. The small

*Das Reich* contingent desperately fought alongside a number of improvised kampfgruppen to hold a firm front facing eastwards, as more than 400 Russian tanks battered at Hube's beleaguered command.

## Strategic withdrawal

Hube and Manstein, however, were determined not to repeat the mistakes made at Stalingrad, which had signed the death warrant of the Sixth Army. They first of all refused to follow Hitler's orders and declare the pocket a "fortress", one that had to be defended to the last man. Hube's pocket was going to be a "mobile pocket" – it would keep moving so the Russians would not be able to trap it, and then concentrate their forces against it.

For more than two weeks Hube kept his army moving southwards, and then westwards to keep the Russians guessing about the exact location of his divisions. Air supply was organized properly, with each division having its own Luftwaffe team who set up improvised airstrips each day. Fuel and ammunition were flown in and the wounded evacuated. By this stage of the war the

Luftwaffe had finally mastered this type of operation, and the air bridge provided Hube's men with just enough supplies for them to keep fighting and moving. The continual movement was also good for morale, and Hube's army did not suffer any of the panics that were seen in the Cherkassy Pocket.

The obvious escape route for Hube's men was to head south, where a number of bridges over the River Dniester into Romania remained open. Zhukov therefore concentrated the bulk of his tanks against these crossings, rather than reinforcing the eastward-facing defences of his pincers. Manstein devised a plan for Hube to attack directly westwards, cutting through the Russian lines to escape and meet up with rescue forces moving east.

Hitler hated the plan because it gave up huge amounts of territory. For days he sat on his hands and refused to make a decision. On 24 March Manstein threatened to issue the breakout orders anyway, unless Hitler agreed to his plan. On this rare occasion the Führer backed down. Field Marshal Manstein got his freedom of movement and

■ *Below:* The snow-covered steppe provided little cover for dismounted Waffen-SS panzergrenadiers, whose task was to hold the Eastern Front together.

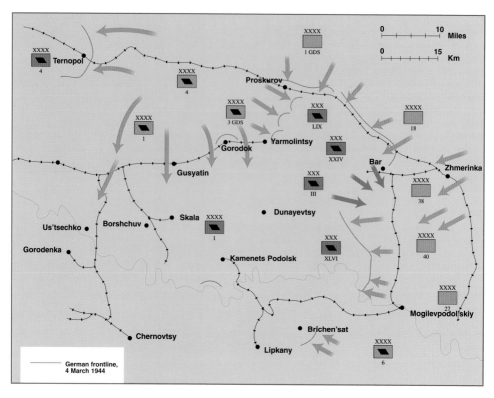

XXXX
1 GDS

0          10
|—+—+—+—| Miles

0          15
|—+—+—+—+—| Km

XXXX
4
Ternopol

XXXX
4
Proskurov

XXXX
3 GDS

XXX
LIX

XXXX
18

XXXX
1

Gorodok

Yarmolintsy

XXX
XXIV

Bar

Zhmerinka

Gusyatin

XXX
III

XXX
38

Skala

XXXX
1

Dunayevtsy

Us'tsechko    Borshchuv

Gorodenka

Kamenets Podolsk

XXX
XLVI

XXXX
40

XXXX
27
Mogilevpodol'skiy

Chernovtsy

Brichen'sat

Lipkany

XXXX
6

————— German frontline,
4 March 1944

■ *Above:* **German units in the Kamenets Podolsk Pocket, March 1944.**

his reinforcements – II SS Panzer Corps. It would begin to move to the Eastern Front from France immediately, with the two well-equipped but unblooded Waffen-SS Divisions: the 9th *Hohenstaufen* and the 10th *Frundsberg* Panzer Divisions.

Inside the pocket, two assault groups were formed to batter past the Soviet defences. The *Leibstandarte*, then part of Kampfgruppe *Mauss*, fell back from its positions on the western flank of the pocket and deployed as part of the flank guard. As part of Corps Group *von Chevallerei*, the élite Waffen-SS division helped hold open the escape corridor for almost 12 days against repeated attacks by the Soviet Third Guards Tank Army. The *Das Reich* Division stayed as the rearguard on the eastern edge of the pocket.

Manstein's deception plan worked. Zhukov did not realize what was happening until it was too late, and he was only able to move one tank corps northwards in an attempt to stop the breakout. By 4 April

1944, the army's 1st and 6th Panzer Divisions were poised to attack the last line of Soviet troops blocking their escape route.

Central to Manstein's breakout plan was the deployment of II SS Panzer Corps to punch a corridor through from the west and take the pressure off Hube's hard-pressed troops in the pocket. On paper, II SS Panzer Corps was a formidable force, but its leaders and soldiers were largely untried in combat. Their commander, SS-Obergruppenführer Willi Bittrich, was one of the most professional officers in the Waffen-SS and he is most famous for the destruction of the British 1st Airborne Division at Arnhem in September 1944. Many of his divisional and regimental commanders were very raw, even though the individual soldiers of the corps showed plenty of Waffen-SS fighting spirit. Bittrich's corps boasted an impressive array of weaponry, with *Hohenstaufen* fielding 21 Panthers, 38 Panzer IVs, 44 StuG IIIs and 12 Marder self-propelled antitank guns, while *Frundsberg* could put 44 Panzer IVs and 49 StuG IIIs into action.

By 3 April, Bittrich's men had finished unloading their tanks from trains in Lvov, and the following day they moved forward into action. The weather was terrible, with thaws one day followed by heavy snow the next. For the first day of the operation, the Army 506th Heavy Panzer Battalion took the lead with its Tiger Is battering away through a large pak-front of antitank guns. Now the *Frundsberg* Division took over the advance for the final 32km (20 miles) to Hube's men. It then immediately ran into a concealed pak-front, and so the division's reconnaissance unit was sent forward to pinpoint the enemy gun pit and bunker positions. Panzers were then brought up to blast the enemy antitank guns one-by-one. Soon the tanks were rolling eastwards again, with the divisional commander, SS-Gruppenführer Karl von Treuenfeld, leading the advance with the first panzer company. He decided that the link-up could be achieved sooner if a direct route across country was taken. At first the move looked like a typical daring Waffen-SS tactic, but within the space of a couple of hours Treuenfeld's tanks were strung out across several kilometres of muddy quagmire. The Waffen-SS general managed to get through to Hube's 6th Panzer Division with five tanks, but he was soon cut off from his division by a massive Soviet infantry attack. The Waffen-SS tank crews often had to fight dismounted from their bogged-in panzers to deal with Soviet tank-hunting squads that lurked in the woods and forests along the column's route. Bittrich came forward to sort out the mess. He organized the destruction of another pak-front, and the advance continued. By 6 April Bittrich had cleared the Soviet infantry brigades in the woods around the town of Buchach, which was the objective of Hube's columns. A supply column with 610 tonnes (600 tons) of fuel then moved down the corridor to refuel Hube's tanks and trucks, which were almost running on vapour. Over the next three days

all the trapped German divisions were able to pass safely into the area held by II SS Panzer Corps. The rescue operation was a major success for Manstein, but the Führer saw it entirely differently. "Wars are not won with brilliantly organized retreats," ranted Hitler. The "saviour of the Eastern Front" was relieved and replaced by Field Marshal Walter Model, who had a reputation for issuing "fight to the last man and bullet" orders. He was more to Hitler's liking.

Attention now turned to tidying up the new frontline, where dozens of small German detachments had been cut off. On 11 April, the *Hohenstaufen* Division was ordered to spearhead the rescue of 4000 Germans trapped in Ternopol. The operation was far from a success. On the first day the division got stuck in another quagmire, and then ran into heavy Soviet resistance. Model was far from impressed by the military professionalism of the Waffen-SS staff officers running the rescue mission, and ordered the division's panzer regiment to be placed under the command of an experienced army officer. The attack got moving again and pushed to within 8km (five miles) of the trapped troops. This time the Soviet ring held. The garrison attempted to break out but was massacred in the process. Only 53 men made it through to the Waffen-SS's lines.

The desperate state of the Eastern Front meant that even the remnants of the *Wiking* Division were mustered to fight in support of the rescue effort. Many soldiers still did not even have personal small arms after losing them in the Korsun/Cherkassy Pocket. Fortunately, the division had just been augmented by a fresh armoured regiment with 79 Panthers, which had been forming in Germany since December 1943. The division was committed to an operation to relieve the cut-off town of Kowel on the Ukrainian-Polish border, which had been surrounded by a Soviet spearhead since mid-March. The attack was ill-fated from the start, with *Wiking*'s ammunition supply train being blown up by an artillery shell.

> ### On 11 April, the Hohenstaufen *Division was ordered to spearhead the rescue of 4000 Germans*

Wiking's no-nonsense commander, Gille, soon got a grip on the situation and personally led an assault force through the Soviet lines to break the siege. For several days he was trapped in the city, after a Russian counterattack severed the Waffen-SS corridor. Gille's men fought furiously to re-open a link to their commander, and the trapped garrison was finally relieved on 6 April. It was a victory of sorts, but the division had suffered many casualties, not just killed but also wounded, which meant the loss of veterans to hospitals and dressing stations. Replacements, if they were available at all, were poor by comparison.

On the southern wing of Army Group South, the *Totenkopf* Division was fighting a desperate rearguard battle around Kirovograd as the Eighth Army fell back to the River Dniester. In a move to pre-empt Soviet spearheads from seizing vital bridges on the German escape route into Romania, the *Totenkopf* Division was ordered to move back from the front to set up a new defensive line in the Eighth Army's rear communications zone. The urgency of the situation meant that Waffen-SS divisions' combat units were loaded into Me 232 Giant transport aircraft and flown on 11 March to their new positions. As the Eighth Army fell back in some disarray, many of its divisions passed through the *Totenkopf*'s lines. However, the Soviet advance soon forced the latter back, too. For most of April, it fell back into Romania and on several occasions had to fight desperate actions to avoid being trapped in pockets.

By May 1944, the Ukraine, which the Führer had been desperate to hold no matter what the cost, had been cleared of German forces, and within a few days the Crimea had also fallen. A succession of massive Soviet offensives had literally smashed their way through Manstein's Army Group South.

Throughout these offensives the Waffen-SS panzer divisions were in the thick of the action. They mounted counterattack after counterattack in the face of overwhelming odds, until they were down to almost their last tanks. In the end, though, Waffen-SS *élan* could not compensate for overwhelming superiority in both tanks and artillery. Ultimate defeat now seemed inevitable.

> ## The Totenkopf *Division was fighting a desperate rearguard battle around Kirovograd*

■ *Above:* **Panther tanks from the army's *Grossdeutschland* Panzergrenadier Division go into action supporting infantry. The division often fought alongside the Waffen-SS during the 1943–44 winter campaign.**

■ *Left:* By the spring of 1944, the *Totenkopf* Division was defending the borders of Romania from heavy Soviet pressure. Here, StuG IIIs go into action during a counterattack.

■ *Below:* *Leibstandarte* Panzer IVs gather for another desperate attack to break the Soviet ring around the Kamenets Podolsk Pocket.

# CHAPTER 4

# CARNAGE AT CAEN

## The 12th SS Panzer Division and the defence of Caen.

I n its billets northwest of Paris, the men of the *Hitlerjugend* Division could clearly hear the waves of Allied bombers passing overhead on the morning of 6 June 1944. This performance was heavier than usual. Throughout the early hours of the morning, a steady stream of phone calls alerted the division to the fact that parachute landings were taking place all over Normandy. The divisional commander, 36-year-old SS-Brigadeführer Fritz Witt, put his command on alert. Commanders frantically roused their troops from bed, and reconnaissance parties were formed, ready for any move to counter the invasion.

In the German High Command, confusion reigned. No one was sure where the Allies had landed or in what strength. Rommel, Rundstedt and Hitler all prevaricated, fearing the landing in Normandy was just a feint to distract attention from an assault in the Pas de Calais, or in the mouth of the Somme. A reconnaissance force was sent to the coast south of the Somme at 02:30 hours but the rest of the *Hitlerjugend* Division had to wait for orders. Reports were coming in every couple of minutes, but there was still no concrete information on the Allied attack.

At 05:00 hours orders were issued for the division to begin concentrating at Lisieux in eastern Normandy. It took several hours for the troops to get on the road, and they spent the rest of the day moving westwards under relentless Allied air attack. Swarms of fighter-bombers – "Jagdbombers" or "Jabos" as they were known to the German panzer crews – were scouting ahead of the Allied bridgehead

■ *Left:* A smashed Panzer IV in Caen, which was turned into a bloody battleground strewn with rubble and wrecked tanks.

**■ *Above:* An award ceremony for *Hitlerjugend* Division members involved in the fighting around Caen.**

twisted and smoking wreckage. Refugee columns clogged the roads, and this was responsible for further hindering the movement of German troops towards Normandy. As a result of these obstacles, it would be nightfall before the division found itself anywhere near striking distance of the Allied bridgehead.

### The Allies have landed

The German High Command was still locked in confusion about what to do with the panzer reserves. By mid-afternoon on 6 June it was clear that the Normandy landing was in fact no feint. Although the Germans did not have precise information, Allied records showed that 55,000 men were firmly established ashore in five main bridgeheads. Only in the late afternoon were the first orders for counterattacks issued to the panzer reserves. The 21st Panzer Division was already in

on the lookout for German columns. Some 20 vehicles were destroyed and more than 80 *Hitlerjugend* soldiers killed or wounded in the attacks. More important than the materiel and human losses was the delay caused as the Waffen-SS columns had to stop, take cover and weave their way past

**■ *Left:* To reach the battlefield around Caen, *Hitlerjugend* Division troops spent almost two days on the road from their assembly areas.**

**■ *Right:* Allied fighter-bombers harassed the *Hitlerjugend* columns as they moved towards the Normandy battle front.**

■ *Above:* The
*Hitlerjugend*'s
Panzer IVs arrived
west of Caen on
the morning of 7
June to spearhead
the division's
counterattack.

action north of Caen against the British bridgeheads. Accordingly, the *Hitlerjugend* and *Panzer Lehr* Divisions were ordered to move against the British beaches. They were under the command of "Sepp" Dietrich's I SS Panzer Corps.

The *Leibstandarte* Division remained in Belgium to counter the threat of an Allied landing in the Pas de Calais, the region which so dogged Hitler. In the meantime, the *Das Reich* and the 17th SS Panzergrenadier Divisions began moving northwards from southwest France. Despite their determination, it would be at least a week before they managed to reach the invasion front. It would also be six days until Hitler finally agreed to release II SS Panzer Corps from the Eastern Front in order that it might return to

Normandy. Far from being able to hammer the Allies with a decisive, knock-out blow, the Germans ended up committing their reserves piecemeal in a desperate bid to shore up a crumbling front.

While Dietrich was easily able to establish contact with his old comrade, Witt, he nevertheless had great problems in trying to link up with the 21st Panzer Division or the remnants of the infantry divisions resisting the British north of the large Norman city of Caen.

Dietrich and other staff officers from the Waffen-SS criss-crossed the German front in order to try to pull together some sort of cohesion. All during the night they worked out various formulae for counterattack plan after counterattack plan. But all of their

> *The Germans committed their reserves piecemeal in a desperate bid to shore up a crumbling front*

plans were rapidly overtaken by events. The commander of the 21st Panzer Division could not be found at his command post, and this was to further frustrate plans to mount a joint attack with the *Hitlerjugend* Division.

Of even more concern was the fact that the arrival of the *Hitlerjugend* Division was still stalled because of the chaotic conditions on the roads. The *Panzer Lehr* Division was even further behind, and would not arrive at the front for days. In the meantime, thousands more Allied troops and tanks were rapidly pouring ashore.

The planned mass panzer attack for the following day had to be scrapped. The most that could be expected was for the *Hitlerjugend* Division to go in, with support from 21st Panzer. The first Kampfgruppe of

the *Hitlerjugend* Division to reach the front was based on the 25th SS Panzergrenadier Regiment, commanded by the famous SS-Standartenführer Kurt "Panzer" Meyer.

## Kurt "Panzer" Meyer

Only 34 years old, Meyer was an aggressive and determined officer who would claim fame for being the youngest German divisional commander of World War II. He would also later be accused of being the perpetrator of war crimes because of the merciless killing of Canadian prisoners of war during the coming battle.

Supreme self-confidence – which, some said, bordered on arrogance – was Meyer's trademark, and when he arrived at the 21st Panzer's headquarters during the early hours of 7 June in order to coordinate the coming

■ *Below:* A *Hitlerjugend* Panzer IV rumbles through Caen. Note the armoured "skirt' to defeat Allied antitank rockets.

■ *Right:* To protect themselves from Allied naval gunfire, *Hitlerjugend* panzergrenadiers had rapidly to dig themselves trench networks and bunkers.

attack, he did not win any friends. He took one look at the situation map and left the army officers in no doubt as to how totally unimpressed he was by their assessment of the threat posed by the Allied forces in the Normandy bridgehead.

"Little fish! We'll throw them back into the sea in the morning." For all his bravado, they could be absolutely sure that Meyer was not joking, either.

Meyer was to push forward on the left flank of the 21st Panzer, after forming up on the western edge of Caen itself. His objective was simple: to reach the coast. By first light, only a few companies of the 25th Regiment were in place on the start-line, with the remainder still moving around the southern suburbs of Caen. In the meantime, the petrol shortages and traffic chaos meant that the 26th SS Panzergrenadier Regiment and the *Hitlerjugend*'s Panther tank battalion would not be in position to attack at the earliest until the following day.

This was to be a worrying time for Meyer as he surveyed the battle front from his command post in the Ardennes abbey, 4.8km (3 miles) outside Caen. At 10:00 hours, his Panzer IV battalion with 50 tanks finally arrived, followed by more of his Waffen-SS panzergrenadiers.

The attack was fixed for 16:00 hours, with two panzergrenadier units advancing line abreast. They were to be supported in

■ *Left:* The *Hitlerjugend*'s first battles in Normandy were run by, left to right, Kurt "Panzer" Meyer, Fritz Witt and Max Wünsche.

■ *Right:* Hundreds of Canadian Shermans were thrown into action against the meagre defence lines of the *Hitlerjugend* Division.

their efforts by large numbers of heavy tanks and artillery.

During the early afternoon, Meyer watched from the Abbey's high tower as the Canadian 3rd Division – which was known to contain three full infantry brigades and was backed by hundreds of tanks – started to form up for a major attack. Blissfully unaware that the *Hitlerjugend* Division was in its path, the Canadian 9th Brigade and a regiment of tanks began their advance. To observers, they looked as unthreatening as a unit which was on a training exercise during peacetime.

Making a split-second decision, Meyer junked his deliberate attack plan and instead decided to lay a devastating ambush for the Allied force. By now this force had bypassed one of his advance panzergrenadier units and was heading deep into the German rear with Carpiquet airfield as its objective. All of Meyer's 88mm-armed tanks and antitank guns which were in hull-down positions on a ridge near the abbey were ordered to hold their fire until the Canadian 9th Brigade and the tanks drove into the centre of Meyer's killing zone. The Panzer IV companies were ordered to move quickly along the hedge-lined roads before taking up vantage fire positions on the flanks of the Canadian line of advance.

### Panzer power strikes

Meyer waited until the Canadians were within 200m (219yd) of his lines before giving the order "Achtung panzer – marsche!" Panzer crews powered up their engines and moved into position.

Fire started raining down on the Canadian brigade. Stuart and Sherman tanks began to explode after taking devastating hits from the *Hitlerjugend* panzers. Then Meyer's I Battalion of panzergrenadiers was launched into the shell-shocked remains of the Canadian 9th Brigade.

The battle lasted for six hours as the two forces became intermingled. Company sized groups of Canadians were surrounded by Meyer's troops in the small Normandy villages. Many fought to the last man, while others surrendered when they ran out of ammunition. Heavy Canadian artillery caused many German casualties that had to be evacuated on the backs of Panzer IVs. A Canadian counterattack now regained some of the lost ground, so Meyer ordered his two remaining panzergrenadier battalions into action. II Battalion with three companies of Panzer IVs led the way in a tight wedge formation. This restored the situation and the Canadians were soon in retreat.

The panzer battalion command group now stumbled into a troop of Shermans and were killed. I Battalion, with one Panzer IV company, pushed forward into a sector held by British troops of the Royal Ulster Rifles. The two forces soon became intermingled in the village of Cambes. British Sherman tanks shot up German gun positions before being knocked out by Panzerfaust teams, while Panzer IVs suffered heavy losses from Allied antitank guns. Both sides now pulled back to defensive positions on either side of Cambes.

Meyer was all set to push forward when he spotted another Canadian brigade moving south around his right flank. The 21st Panzer Division's attack had still not started and Meyer was afraid his flank would be turned. His Kampfgruppe was just not strong enough to take on all of the 3rd Canadian Division, so he reluctantly called a halt to his attack. As night fell, the 25th Regiment adopted defensive positions and easily saw off a series of night probes by the Canadians.

Two Canadian regiments – the North Nova Scotia Highlanders and Sherbrooke Fusiliers – lost more than 500 men killed, wounded or captured, as well as 28 tanks destroyed or damaged, during the day's engagement. Meyer lost some 300 casualties and 9 tanks. At the time, many of Meyer's troops were despondent, as they had failed to reach their objective. Given the odds, however, they had achieved an amazing result, stopping the Canadian advance in its tracks and thereby thwarting General Sir Bernard Montgomery's plans to seize Caen on that same day.

> *Stuart and Sherman tanks started to explode after taking devastating hits from* Hitlerjugend *panzers*

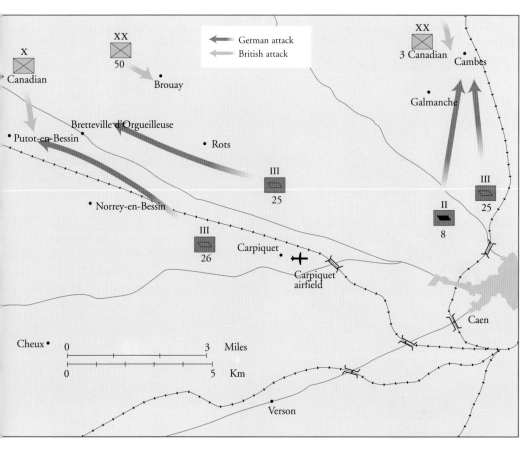

German attack
British attack

X
Canadian

XX
50

Brouay

Bretteville d'Orgueilleuse

Putot-en-Bessin

Rots

III
25

Norrey-en-Bessin

III
26

Carpiquet

Carpiquet
airfield

XX
3 Canadian

Cambes

Galmanche

III
25

II
8

Caen

Cheux

0          3   Miles

0          5   Km

Verson

■ *Above:* **The** **Hitlerjugend** **successfully** **defeated a number** **of Allied attacks to** **the north and** **northwest of Caen** **in early June 1944.**

The following day saw Meyer forced to consolidate his small force until the rest of the division was in a position to attack. Out on the left flank, the *Hitlerjugend*'s reconnaissance battalion tried to link up with any German units still putting up resistance, but Meyer's flank was effectively hanging in open air. The halftrack-mounted reconnaissance troops had a lively day, skirmishing with British troops and tanks of the Durham Light Infantry and 4th/7th Dragoon Guards, convincing them that the German front was far stronger than it really was.

Pushing westwards from Caen, small *Hitlerjugend* patrols in SdKfz 250 half-tracks or SdKfz 234 eight-wheeled armoured cars were trying to find out the extent of the Allied advance southwards. Operating in small groups, the German vehicles soon

started engaging Allied advance patrols. By the evening, the battalion was pulled back to form a firm defensive line to cover the deployment of the 26th Panzergrenadier Regiment.

On 8 June, SS-Oberstürmbannführer Wilhelm Mohnke's 26th Regiment was to attack at first light. This was Mohnke's return to combat duty after almost three years recovering from the loss of a foot in Yugoslavia and serving in a number of administrative jobs. His comrades were watching closely to see if he held up under the pressure. The division's Panther tank battalion was still delayed by fuel shortages, so his three panzergrenadier battalions would go into the attack with no tank support.

Mohnke's task was to drive back the Allied units which had been detected by the

■ *Above:* British infantry soon joined the battle against the *Hitlerjugend*, alongside the Canadian 3rd Infantry Division. This is a machine gunner from the Durham Light Infantry.

reconnaissance battalion as they moved forward on the extreme left of the *Hitlerjugend* Division's flank. Mohnke's men proceeded forward on foot, supported only by SdKfz 251/22 armoured halftracks armed with 75mm guns.

First into action at dawn was the 26th Regiment's I Battalion. Its men were tasked with seizing the village of Norrey-en-Bessin. Without armour support, the attack soon found itself bogged down. When the lead panzergrenadier companies were caught in the open by Canadian machine-gun, mortar and artillery fire, the Germans had to admit

defeat. After many of the company and platoon commanders had been killed or wounded, the Waffen-SS attack was eventually repulsed.

In the centre of the regiment's attack was the II Battalion, which had been assigned the village of Putot-en-Bessin as its objective. Due to strong artillery support, the II Battalion was able to reach the village and surround three companies of the Canadian Royal Winnipeg Rifles inside a few buildings. The Canadians tried to escape, but the Waffen-SS killed or captured most of them. The British 24th Lancers counterattacked in response to the success of the Germans, getting in amongst the panzergrenadiers. More than 40 Germans were captured in this foray before the III Battalion's self-propelled anti-tank company intervened with its Marders and drove the British off.

As dusk was falling, the 7th Canadian Brigade launched a major counterattack, with heavy artillery and tank support. Under massive pressure, the II Battalion pulled out of Putot-en-Bessin, losing some 100 men in the action.

Meanwhile Mohnke's armoured personnel carrier-mounted panzergrenadier unit, III Battalion, went into attack on the extreme left flank of his regiment. It rapidly relieved a badly shot-up panzergrenadier battalion of the *Panzer Lehr* Division in Brouay and then spent the day fending off one attack after the other from British tanks.

## Outgunned by the British

Out on the *Hitlerjugend*'s extreme left flank, the reconnaissance battalion found itself outgunned by the British 8th Armoured Brigade. Pin-pointed by British scouts, the battalion was now targeted by three artillery regiments and two battleships. The battalion's command post was wiped out in a single salvo, and its companies were also targeted, with total losses running to 80 men.

As the evening began, it was Meyer's 25th Regiment's turn to go forward on the attack. The offensive would enjoy the support of the *Hitlerjugend*'s Panther tank battalion. In a daring night attack, Meyer punched through the Canadian lines and surrounded a regimental headquarters based inside the village of Bretteville d'Orgueilleuse. This attack, which was westward from his position, was intended to strike at the exposed flank of the Canadian brigade which was counterattacking Mohnke's regiment.

The 25th Regiment's reconnaissance company followed up on its motorcycles, close behind the two companies of tanks, and they were to storm Canadian trenches after the panzer assault. Panzergrenadiers were then to mop up the Canadian position. In characteristic fashion, Meyer went into

> *In characteristic fashion, Meyer went into battle on a motorcycle side car, his way of motivating his men*

■ *Left:* The fighting outside Caen was intense, with heavy casualties on both sides. This soldier from the Durham Light Infantry has been lucky.

battle riding on a motorcycle side car, his way of motivating his men to give their all, but showing how impetuous the 32-year-old leader could be in the heat of battle.

As they approached the village, the Panthers fanned out into attack formation and gathered speed. A wall of antitank gun-fire hit them as they got to within 200m (219yd) of the village, knocking out several tanks. Spurred on by Meyer's presence, the tanks started to blast apart the village, with burning tanks and buildings turning night into day. The Canadians fired their salvos of parachute flares above the German tanks, silhouetting them, thereby providing excellent targets as well as temporarily blinding the Panther crews. Meyer now changed his tactics, sending groups of tanks and panzergrenadiers to penetrate the village from the north and south, thus avoiding the heavy antitank gunfire.

The Canadians retreated into a series of fortified strongpoints to try to hold off the attack. Meyer's Panthers were able to get into the village, where they proceeded to shoot up Canadian bunkers and trucks.

In a crazy night battle, some 22 Panthers circled the Canadian command post of the Regina Rifles Regiment, with Meyer darting in between them in his motorcycle! The I Battalion had not been able to penetrate the Canadian defences, leaving the Panthers largely unsupported. In the end Canadian PIAT bazookas and antitank guns firing new sabot rounds knocked out six of the Panthers, so Meyer reluctantly called off the attack as dawn was breaking.

Small groups of German motorcyclists had managed to get into the village, and were eventually able to make their escape back to German lines. Meyer's foray had been an expensive exercise, and had left 155 men dead, wounded or prisoners. The commander of the *Hitlerjugend*'s panzer regiment, Max Wünsche, had gone along for the ride on a borrowed tank, but for all his bravado, had not been as lucky as Meyer and had ended up wounded.

> *Canadian infantry joined in, machine-gunning the survivors as they made their escape on foot*

■ *Right:* Canadian infantry and tank reserves were thrown into the battle in an attempt to overwhelm the *Hitlerjugend* defenders of Caen.

■ *Above:* Allied tank and infantry cooperation left much to be desired, and hampered attempts to open a gap in the *Hitlerjugend*'s lines.

Allied pressure on Mohnke's Regiment continued during 9 June, with a series of attacks by both British and Canadian troops. The 8th Armoured Brigade continued to probe into the *Hitlerjugend*'s reconnaissance battalion, which now had been joined by a Panther company, attached to beef-up its firepower. They traded fire with British Shermans all day, but were not able to hold back their advance. Only the arrival of elements of the *Panzer Lehr* Division could neutralize this threat to *Hitlerjugend*'s flank.

Meyer tried again with another raid by the Panther battalion which took place early on in the afternoon, but lost seven tanks to Canadian antitank fire. He sent a company of 12 tanks forward without infantry and artillery, expecting the surprise and shock effect to unnerve the defenders who were now dug-in in the village of Norrey-en-Bessin. The tanks formed a long line and headed out across open fields towards their objective when, one by one, the Panthers started to fall victim to Canadian tanks in ambush positions. Each Panther caught fire,

and all the crew who escaped were badly burned. Canadian infantry then joined in, machine-gunning the survivors as they made their escape on foot. The whole episode was a dismal failure, with 15 men dead and 20 badly wounded.

The failure of the attack was a major problem for the *Hitlerjugend* Division, because it left a Canadian strongpoint jutting southwards into the line between the 25th and 26th Regiments. During the early hours of 10 June, the division's pioneer battalion was to go into action to neutralize the position. German pioneers were considered élite infantry, specializing in assault operations and, as a result, great gains were expected to be made from their attack.

Under cover of darkness, the pioneers tried to approach the Canadian position in silence, but they were soon detected. Heavy mortar and artillery fire began raining down on the exposed pioneers. They managed to reach the edge of the village before the attack stalled. For most of the following day the men were pinned down, finding themselves

■ *Above:* The USS *Nevada* and other Allied battleships made life very uncomfortable for the German defenders in Normandy, raining down a constant stream of high explosives far inland.

unable either to advance or to retreat. By late afternoon, the pioneers managed to pull back, but they were forced to leave 80 dead or wounded behind. Allied naval gunfire support continued to pound the *Hitlerjugend* Division, and it was to have a devastating effect as 14in and 16in shells rained down on Caen. The use of altitude fuses meant the Allied shelling resulted in hot shrapnel raining down on German positions. When not actually fighting, Meyer had his men digging bunkers, trenches, artillery gun pits and panzer shelters. By digging large scrapes to drive their tanks into, the panzer crews protected their vehicles from the unrelenting barrages which

■ *Right:* With German defences solidifying, the Allies had quickly to rethink their strategy and tactics at Caen.

■ *Right:* British
General Bernard
Montgomery
(standing in car)
visits the Normandy
bridgehead in early
June to work out his
next move.

■ *Right:* British General Bernard Montgomery (standing in car) visits the Normandy bridgehead in early June to work out his next move.

smashed radio antenna, destroyed sighting optics or, in some extreme cases, ripped off tank turrets.

### Firepower mismatch

Time and time again, Dietrich tried to muster his panzer divisions for a corps-level counterattack, but he was constantly having to reorganize his forces to plug holes in the front. The *Panzer Lehr* Division had still not arrived in strength, leaving the *Hitlerjugend* Division to hold the line to the west of Caen for another day. It was reinforced by the arrival of I SS Panzer Corps' artillery regiment, but this boost did little to even out the mismatch between German and Allied firepower on the Normandy Front.

The Canadians were now joined by the British 50th Division for a major attack on the afternoon of 11 June. The reconnaissance battalion again proved its worth as a hard-hitting mobile strike force. A company of *Hitlerjugend* Panthers and the division's reconnaissance battalion raced to block their line of advance. Holding their fire until the British tanks had raced ahead of their infantry, machine gunners in the reconnaissance halftracks then raked the ranks of the Green Howards Regiment. Lying in ambush, the Panthers picked off the British Shermans of the 4th/7th Dragoon Guards from a hilltop firing line. The British attack faltered when one Sherman that had penetrated to with a few yards of the German battalion's command post was knocked out by a 75mm antitank gun. The arrival of the reserve Panther company sent the British reeling backwards. The British lost 250 men and seven tanks in withering German fire.

At the same time, the Canadian 2nd Armoured Brigade had been launched against Mohnke's regiment. The brunt of the attack fell on the divisional pioneer battalion, which was now holding the line south of Norrey-en-Bessin. A regiment of Shermans rolled forward, loaded with infantrymen on their rear decks. The pioneers were soon locked in fierce hand-to-hand combat. Shermans were stalked by German Panzerfaust teams through village streets and country lanes.

A Panzer IV company was moved forward from a reserve position to a hill which overlooked the Canadian line of advance. Hitting the Canadians in the flank, some 46 Shermans were soon burning fiercely in the

> *Shermans were stalked by German Panzerfaust teams through village streets and country lanes*

Normandy fields. Not surprisingly, Shermans were soon nicknamed Ronsons, after the wartime cigarette lighter, because of their alarming ability to burn.

The Panzers now charged the confused mass of Canadians, sending them running back to their start line. Almost 200 Germans were killed or wounded, along with three tanks destroyed, in the desperate battle.

As this battle was taking place, the 40th Canadian Armoured Regiment, along with a commando unit, were launched against the village of Rots, which was at that point held by a composite Kampfgruppe of divisional escort troops and a company of Panthers. Although more than 15 Shermans were knocked out, ultimately the attackers were far too strong for the defenders. They slowly fell back through the streets of the village, inflicting more than 100 casualties on the Allies as they went.

By nightfall, the Canadians were in complete control of the village. During the fighting, just under 70 Germans were killed or wounded, and one Panther tank was knocked out.

In four days of bitter fighting the *Hitlerjugend* Division had effectively brought the Allied advance to a halt on the outskirts of Caen. For a unit in action for the first time, it had put up a remarkable performance. Although many *Hitlerjugend* troopers were despondent that they had not driven the Allies back into the sea, given the odds they faced, they had achieved far more than could be expected. Caen had been Montgomery's objective for the attacks on 7 and 8 June, but the city remained firmly in German hands. The Allied commander would soon try different tactics to take it. One result of the fighting for Caen was a realization by Hitler and the High Command that Normandy was in fact the main Allied invasion front. After Caen, the Führer was finally forced to agree to change his tactics, and accordingly he ordered the *Leibstandarte* Division to move up to the front from its base in Belgium.

Similarly, II SS Panzer Corps was recalled from the Eastern Front on 12 June in order to assist its comrades in their efforts to counter the Allied invasion.

## War criminals on trial

The fighting which took place in the fields and villages to the northwest of Caen was some of the most violent and brutal to be seen during the Normandy campaign. The *Hitlerjugend* Division lost over 1000 dead, wounded or missing in these engagements, while the Canadians alone lost nearly 3000 of their men. Equipment losses were equally heavy on both sides. In those violent first engagements between the *Hitlerjugend* and Canadian troops, little quarter was ever given. As a result, in the bloody aftermath, accusations flew back and forth that many prisoners had been executed by both sides.

Meyer and a number of his officers were charged with war crimes after the war had ended. Meyer was charged with being responsible for five incidents on 7 and 8 June which involved the deaths of 41 Canadian prisoners. He was also charged with issuing orders to his division to give no quarter to prisoners. Seven other *Hitlerjugend* Division officers were investigated for war crimes, involving the deaths of at least 134 Canadian prisoners. After long trials and appeals, Meyer and two others were found guilty of all or some of the charges and sentenced to death. Meyer later had his death sentence stayed, but his two comrades were not so lucky and they faced the hangman's noose in 1948. On his release, Meyer launched a campaign to clear his reputation as well as redeem that of his beloved *Hitlerjugend* Division.

Both sides produced accounts of the unlawful killing of prisoners, the Waffen-SS men claiming that they were subjected to "victor's justice" in show trials. In one famous case, men of the *Hitlerjugend* claimed they had executed 3 Canadians in reprisal for the deaths of 10 German soldiers tied to a British armoured car and machine-gunned. The truth of these events will never be known, but bear testimony to the fact that during the summer of 1944, Normandy had become a brutal killing field.

> *In the bloody aftermath, accusations flew back and forth that prisoners were executed by both sides*

■ *Right:* The *Hitlerjugend* Division held the line north of Caen, but at a terrible price in both men and equipment.

# CHAPTER 5

# VILLERS-BOCAGE

## The exploits of Germany's top panzer ace, Michael Wittmann.

With the Canadians and British stalemated in front of Caen by the stalwart defence of the *Hitlerjugend* Division, General Montgomery decided to exploit the gap in the German front. He resolved that this would best be done on the exposed Waffen-SS division's left flank. The *Panzer Lehr* Division was moving into place next to the *Hitlerjugend* after something of a long delay, but in turn its left flank was also exposed, and the Germans had not yet been able to establish a continuous front between the divisions shielding Caen and units fighting the Americans in the western part of Normandy.

Montgomery's answer was Operation Perch. The fresh British 7th Armoured Division was launched southwards around the open left flank of the *Panzer Lehr* Division on 12 June. Its mission was to out-flank the *Panzer Lehr*, then swing around behind it and drive hell for leather through Villers-Bocage towards Caen, trapping both the *Hitlerjugend* and *Panzer Lehr* Divisions. On paper, the plan was very sound; indeed, it was straight out of the Blitzkrieg school of tactics. The execution was flawed, however, and the famous Desert Rats soon found their nemesis in the shape of a single, determined Waffen-SS Tiger I tank commander.

The 55-tonne (54-ton) Tiger I tank had been in service with the Waffen-SS since late 1942. It had first seen action with devastating effect during the heavy fighting around Kharkov on the Eastern Front in February and March 1943. With its 88mm cannon, the Tiger could easily punch through the armour of Soviet T-34s and

■ *Left:* A Tiger I tank of the 101st SS Heavy Panzer Battalion on its way to the Normandy Front to counter the Allied invasion.

Allied Shermans at more than 1500m (1640yd) range. At first the *Leibstandarte*, *Das Reich* and *Totenkopf* Divisions had each been assigned a Tiger I company of some 15 tanks, although the Tiger's notorious unreliability meant that it was often the case that only half of a company's tanks were operational at any one time. These tanks had been used as spearhead units during the Battle of Kursk in July 1943.

> ## The Tiger's unreliability meant that only half a company's tanks were operational at any one time

As a result of the expansion of the Waffen-SS panzer corps in the summer of 1943, it was decided to remove the divisional Tiger companies and form two corps-level heavy tank battalions. These were nominally to have three Tiger I companies, each with

14 tanks each. The continued commitment of the *Leibstandarte*, *Das Reich* and *Totenkopf* on the Eastern Front through the winter of 1943, and into the spring of 1944, meant the two new battalions were not ready for action until just before the invasion of France. The 101st SS Heavy Panzer Battalion itself was assigned to support I SS Panzer Corps, and the 102nd SS Heavy Panzer Battalion worked for the sister corps. They were to provide each of the Waffen-SS corps with a hard-hitting strike force, or a reserve counter-punch.

The 101st SS Battalion had been ordered to Normandy immediately after the Allied invasion, but persistent Allied air raids

■ *Below:* Allied bombing of the French railway and bridge networks meant that Waffen-SS Tigers had to drive from Paris to the front, putting a great strain on the vehicles' temperamental tracks and transmissions.

delayed the advance of its 37 operational tanks. It arrived in I SS Panzer Corps' sector west of Caen on 12 June, just as the *Panzer Lehr* Division was taking up position alongside the *Hitlerjugend* Division.

One of its companies, under the command of 30-year-old SS-Obersturmführer Michael Wittmann, was posted behind the army division and was to be used only as a reserve force. Wittmann was, by June 1944, one of the most highly decorated German tank commanders of the war, boasting the Knight's Cross with Oak Leaves. His kill tally ran to an astronomical 119 tanks, almost all of which were claimed during a particularly successful year serving with the *Leibstandarte*'s Tiger company on the Eastern Front.

Operation Perch got under way during the afternoon of 12 June, with the 22nd Armoured Brigade leading the way. All went well until a single German antitank gun knocked out a British Stuart tank near the village of Livery. Rather than pressing on to exploit the open German flank during the light summer evening, the British commander, Major-General Bobby Erskine, chose to halt for the night. This was turning into no British Blitzkrieg.

### Wittmann on the rampage

Suitably rested, the 7th Armoured Division started out for Villers-Bocage at first light on 13 June and, by 08:00 hours, its advance guard – the task of which had been assigned to the Cromwell tanks of the 4th City of London Yeomanry "Sharpshooters" (4 CLY) – was passing through the town. Another tank unit, the 5th Royal Tank Regiment, a motorized infantry battalion from the Rifle Brigade, as well as assorted antitank and artillery, were in or around the small Norman town under the command of the 22nd Armoured Brigade. 4 CLY's A Squadron halted on a prominent hill feature to the east of the town in order to have a rest and brew some tea!

Watching from a nearby wood was Wittmann, who famously replied when he heard his gunner, Bobby Woll's, comment, "they are acting as if they've won the war already" with the retort: "We're going to prove them wrong."

Wittmann ordered his remaining operational Tigers and a Panzer IV from the *Panzer Lehr* Division to stay behind in their hide while he went on a quick reconnaissance mission into the town. He moved south of the British column which was strung out along the Caen road and, unobserved, was able to penetrate into the town. Four Cromwell tanks of the 4 CLY headquarters troop were parked in the main street, with their crews dismounted, making tea or carrying out minor repairs. Wittmann caught them totally by surprise and three of the British tanks were immediately destroyed as he rampaged along the street. One of the tanks was saved by a quick-thinking driver who slammed his vehicle into reverse and backed into a garden.

■ *Above:* Michael Wittmann was soon to become the most famous Tiger tank commander in the Waffen-SS for his exploits at Villers-Bocage.

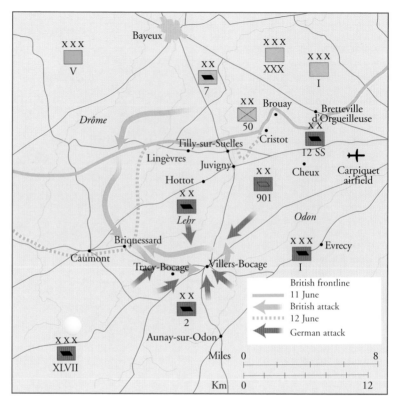

■ *Right:* The plan
for Operation Perch
in June 1944 was
for the British 7th
Armoured Division to
break through at
Villers-Bocage to
trap the *Panzer Lehr*
and *Hitlerjugend*
Divisions.

Cruising down the main street of the town, Wittmann drove past this tank and soon found himself confronted by the whole of 4 CLY's B Squadron. After exchanging several shots with the British tanks, including a 17-pounder-armed Sherman Firefly, Wittmann backed off, reversing away and then turning around. His intention was to rejoin his other Tigers but, driving back down the main street, Wittmann found himself head-to-head with the surviving Cromwell tank that had come out to fight him. The two tanks traded rounds at almost point-blank range. Two British 75mm rounds bounced off the front of Wittmann's Tiger, until one of Woll's 88mm shells found its mark, destroying the British tank. Running short of ammunition, Wittmann pulled back

*Wittmann found himself head-to-head with the surviving Cromwell that had come out to fight*

and rejoined the rest of his company. After they had re-stocked on 88mm rounds, the company set upon the 4 CLY's A Squadron with a vengeance.

Unobserved by the British, Wittmann's Tigers were able to approach their unsuspecting prey from behind. First of all, they knocked out a M3 halftrack at the rear of the British column. This decisive action effectively trapped the British in a sunken road where, unable to move, their tanks and a range of other vehicles were little more than sitting ducks to their German attackers.

After first dealing with the Sherman Fireflys – which alone could threaten the Tigers – Wittmann's tank, helped by the Panzer IV, just drove along the column, picking off the enemy's vehicles one by one.

By 10:30 hours, the 4 CLY battle group had virtually ceased to exist. The surviving troops on Point 213 surrendered at 13:00 hours.

Wittmann alone had accounted for 23 armoured vehicles, out of a total kill of 20 Cromwells, 4 Sherman Fireflys, 3 Stuarts, 3 artillery observer tanks, 16 Bren Gun carriers, 14 M3 halftracks and 2 6-pounder antitank guns. More than 100 British soldiers had been captured and some 62 had been killed. The commanding officer of the 4 CLY, the Viscount Cranley, was later found to be hiding in a wood when German infantry swept the area for prisoners, and he too was captured.

As his tanks were finishing off A Squadron, Wittmann now decided to go after the remainder of the British force in Villers-Bocage itself. 4 CLY's remaining B Squadron had responded to calls for help from its comrades trapped on Point 213, but its men had found the route blocked by the knocked-out Cromwells and a steep railway embankment. A troop of four Cromwells and a Sherman Firefly were then sited in an ambush position in the main square in order to trap any German tanks that might try to push down the main street again for a second attack. A 6-pounder antitank gun was also positioned to fire into the side armour of any tanks which were seen to be driving past the square of the town.

## The British strike back

Unaware of the "Tiger trap" that had been set for him, Wittmann set off into the town, with one of his Tigers and the Panzer IV in close support. The British tanks let Wittmann's Tiger pass by, then the 6-pounder opened up, striking the armoured monster in its vulnerable side armour. A Cromwell got the following Tiger with a similar shot and British infantry with PIAT bazookas opened up as well. The Panzer IV decided to beat a hasty retreat and, blasting at houses known to contain British infantry

■ *Below:* British Cromwell tanks of the 7th Armoured Division were outgunned and outarmoured by the Waffen-SS Tigers. The Cromwell's main armament was a 75mm gun.

■ *Above:* French civilians turned out in their hundreds to welcome the tanks of the 7th Armoured Division as they pushed south towards Villers-Bocage, and a major defeat.

as it went, the tank turned and retreated at full speed down the main street of the town.

At this point the Sherman Firefly pulled out of the square and planted a 17-pounder shell in the engine of the escaping Panzer IV. The German crews bailed out of their tanks and took cover in the now-ruined street. In the ensuing confusion, they were able to make good their escape. To prevent the Germans from recovering their damaged tanks in order to use them later on in the conflict, British troops stuffed petrol-soaked blankets in the tanks' vision ports and set them on fire.

Wittmann now walked more than 7km (4.3 miles) to the headquarters of the *Panzer Lehr* Division. At these headquarters, he briefed the divisional operations officer on the action in Villers-Bocage. He was given command of a company of 15 Panzer IVs and ordered to clear the town of all British troops.

The remainder of Wittmann's tanks – as well as other Tigers from 101st Battalion's 1st Company – had already joined in the fight when he arrived back at the town at about 13:00 hours. The 1st Company Tigers led the attack into the main street of the town. In the meantime, a Kampfgruppe of infantry from the *Panzer Lehr* Division joined the attack.

British infantry had now reinforced the town and, at the mercy of this strengthened force, the German tanks were met by a hail of PIAT bazooka rounds. Antitank grenades – which the British dropped from upper storeys – were to account for at least one of the four Tigers and one Panzer IV destroyed in the battle.

The Tigers which had survived the battle now pulled back, with this action leaving the remainder of the fighting to the *Panzer Lehr* infantry. By 17:00 hours, an exhausted General Erskine gave the order for the 22nd Brigade to pull out of Villers-Bocage. The battered remnants of this force were to take up their positions on a hill to the east. However, they were given no respite and were pressed closely during the night by the German troops. By the following morning, the Germans had severely dented the British force's morale and had managed to inflict more than 100 casualties.

The Germans continued to press forward, with the 101st SS Battalion's Tigers supporting elements of the 2nd Panzer

> *By the following morning, the Germans had managed to inflict more than 100 casualties*

Division. The men of these units were now arriving in accordance with orders, determined to give their full support to their comrades on the Normandy Front.

### Desert Rats withdraw

A full-scale withdrawal of the 7th Armoured Division was now ordered by a panicked Montgomery. The commander was haunted by visions of his once élite division being cut off behind German lines where it would be left to an uncertain fate. Accordingly, at 14:00 hours, more than 300 RAF heavy bombers started raining 1727 tonnes (1700 tons) of bombs on Villers-Bocage to cover the withdrawal of the Desert Rats. A total count of one Waffen-SS Tiger was destroyed and three damaged in this massive airborne raid. The action would also leave 29 Tiger crews as casualties.

Still the Germans pressed the retreating British and, when the 2nd Panzer's reconnaissance battalion hit the 7th Armoured in the flank, Erskine called in fire from 160 British and American heavy guns to allow his men to break contact. One Tiger was knocked out in this fighting. By nightfall on 14 June, the 7th Armoured Division was

■ *Below:* The path of Wittmann's Tiger in the main street of Villers-Bocage.

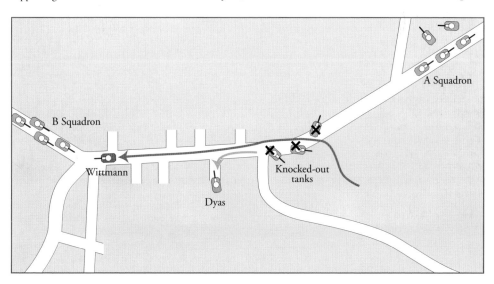

■ *Right:* Wittmann's brief foray into Villers-Bocage left a trail of devastation.

■ *Below:* German armour fell victim to British antitank guns in the village's confined streets.

back at its start-line of two days earlier. It would go down in the annals of history as the unit which suffered the first major Allied defeat of the entire Normandy campaign.

Instead of being a Blitzkrieg, Operation Perch had ended as a shambolic retreat. The materiel losses on the British side were not great and numbered less than 50 tanks. However, during the action, a whole divisional attack had first been thwarted and then decisively thrown back.

Credit for this achievement must surely go to Wittmann, who saw the danger posed by the 22nd Armoured Brigade and was responsible for striking the decisive blow. It was his intervention which gave the *Panzer Lehr* Division's commander – the

redoubtable Fritz Bayerlein – the time he needed to mobilize the counterattack force which was eventually strong enough to drive back the famous Desert Rats.

### Getting Rommel out of Caen

In recognition of his efforts during Operation Perch, on the recommendation of Bayerlein, Wittmann was rewarded with Swords to his Knight's Cross by a grateful Führer. The celebrated Waffen-SS officer was also promoted to the rank of SS-Hauptsturmführer. Smarting in his field headquarters, Montgomery was now preoccupied with devising his next offensive to prise Rommel's men out of Caen. The *Hitlerjugend* would again be the target.

■ *Above:* To cover the Desert Rats' withdrawal, RAF heavy bombers pummelled Villers-Bocage, causing massive damage but inflicting only a handful of casualties on the remaining Germans. This Cromwell was knocked out by the Germans.

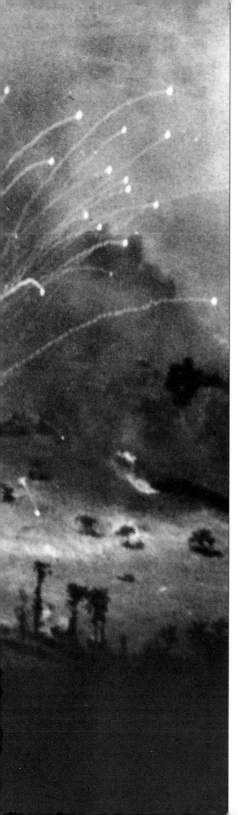

# CHAPTER 6

# PANZER INFERNO

## The defeat of Operation Epsom and the recapture of Hill 112.

**W**ith the blunting of the outflanking movement by the British 7th Armoured Division at Villers-Bocage, General Montgomery had to look again at how he was going to take Caen, and open a route for his armour to break out into the French countryside beyond. The arrival of the *Panzer Lehr* and 2nd Panzer Divisions in the German frontline to the west of Caen effectively closed down the option of any rapid movement by tank forces out of the Allied bridgehead. Any attack would have to punch straight through the German front.

Montgomery now came up with the idea of a corps-level attack. In this manoeuvre, three infantry divisions backed by enormous firepower would create a breach for the newly arrived 11th Armoured Division to exploit. More than 60,000 men, backed by more than 600 tanks and 900 guns, would be thrown into the attack. The objective would be the high ground to the west of Caen, just south of the River Odon. This would be the biggest Allied offensive in Normandy so far.

The Allied bridgehead in Normandy was now firmly secure, with thousands of ships delivering 35,000 men, 6000 vehicles and 25,401 tonnes (25,000 tons) of stores a day onto the French coast. By 17 June there were 557,000 Allied troops, with 81,000 vehicles – including 3200 tanks – ashore. The Germans were also racing to reinforce their armies in Normandy. By mid-June 1944, though, Rommel probably only had half as many men at the front as the Allies and some 859 armoured vehicles.

■ *Left:* A German ammunition dump explodes during an RAF attack, further reducing the ability of Rommel to hold his front together.

■ *Above:* RAF Typhoons operating from forward airbases in Normandy prowled over German frontlines, making any kind of movement in daylight very hazardous.

■ *Left:* German communications links, such as the Paris marshalling yards, were devastated by Allied air raids, making it impossible for reinforcements and supplies to reach the Normandy Front.

■ *Right:* French resistance fighters joined the Allied air effort to interdict German lines of communications.

Aware that the Allies were concentrating on pumping huge amounts of men and materiel ashore into their bridgehead, the German commanders, Rommel and Rundstedt, were constantly engaged in their efforts to muster a strong counterattack force to drive the British and Americans back into the sea.

Great hopes were now placed in the fresh divisions of Paul Hausser's II SS Panzer Corps. This unit was currently *en route* from the Russian Front, and was expected to be available in Normandy in the last week of June 1944.

At the same time, the *Leibstandarte* Division was also – at last – on its way to the front from Belgium, and *Das Reich* and the 17th SS Panzergrenadier Divisions were moving northwards from Toulouse and Bordeaux respectively. It was intended to launch Hausser's corps at the boundary between the British and American bridge-

heads. This move would split the Allies apart and the Germans would then be able to crush each of them in turn.

The German plans, however, were constantly being thwarted by the late arrival of the armour necessary for this job. There was also a lack of infantry, which was needed to allow the panzer divisions already in the line to be pulled back and launched into the counterattack.

It was for these reasons that the few panzer divisions which were stationed in Normandy, such as the *Hitlerjugend*, were still holding the front west of Caen a week after being committed to action. Under a relentless bombardment by hundreds of guns, battleship broadsides and thousands of fighter-bombers, German combat power was being steadily wasted away. The *Hitlerjugend*'s commander, Fritz Witt, succumbed to a naval gunfire barrage on 14 June when his command post was blasted by a huge salvo. Caught by shell splinters as he dived into a bunker, Witt was killed instantly. The 32-year-old Kurt Meyer was immediately appointed in Witt's place, making him the youngest German divisional commander of the war.

Allied bombing of the French railway and bridge network played havoc with Rommel's attempts to bolster his battered front. The only safe way to move men and materiel by rail was under the cover of darkness, and the nearest railheads to the Normandy Front were a good day's drive away, in the western suburbs of Paris. This geographical constraint posed a particular problem for panzer units which had to make long road-marches to the front from railheads, since it put an immense strain on the sensitive tracks, engines and transmissions of their tanks. The damage caused by this rough ride forced many tanks to be left behind, from where they would be collected by their recovery parties.

These were losses that Rommel's small panzer force could ill-afford. As the panzers approached the front, they started to receive attention from Allied fighter-bombers, the dreaded "Jabos", as they were called by the

*Allied bombing played havoc with Rommel's attempts to bolster his battered front*

Germans. As an average, German units lost between 5 percent and 10 percent of their vehicle strength to Allied air attacks or mechanical breakdowns as they moved to Normandy. When the *Leibstandarte* arrived at the front in late June, its panzer battalions had only 75 percent of their tanks fit to fight.

Farther from the front, the activities of the French resistance – blowing up bridges and ambushing isolated German columns – were beginning to play a major part in delaying the arrival of Waffen-SS units. Forced by damage to the railway network to travel mainly by road, the *Das Reich* Division was plagued by resistance attacks. However, the division was hardened by years of fighting in Russia and its officers responded in the way they had in the East: brutally, and without any mercy.

## SS retribution

When the *Das Reich* reconnaissance battalion entered the town of Tulle, it allegedly found the remains of 62 German soldiers who had been mutilated, it was claimed, by some resistance fighters. This act of brutality was said to have taken place after the Germans had surrendered. In response, the *Das Reich* troopers rounded up 99 Frenchmen and hung them from lamp-posts as an example of what would happen if German troops were attacked.

If deterring others was the intention, it failed. Resistance attacks continued apace. Matters came to a head when a *Das Reich* convoy was fired upon near the town of Oradour, killing an SS-Hauptsturmführer. As revenge, the Waffen-SS men ringed the town, rounding up its entire population in the local church, before setting the church on fire. The blaze killed the 548 men, women and children inside the church. One German was killed when a slate fell off a roof and hit him on the head. In the hours that followed, every building in the town was either blown up or set on fire.

This massacre at Oradour was the worst incident of its type in the West to be committed by Waffen-SS troops, although such brutal behaviour was considered routine in the East. Rommel, who had never served in the East, was outraged at the massacre and

■ *Below:* This map shows the German plan to drive a wedge between US and British forces in Normandy, and Montgomery's plan to take Caen, codenamed Operation Epsom. Of the two plans, the British one stood more chance of success given Allied air superiority and their massive materiel advantages.

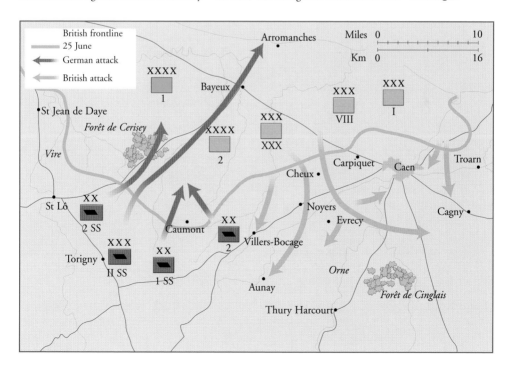

■ *Right:* German
logistics could
barely cope with
moving troops to
Normandy, let alone
building up the
supplies needed to
drive the Allies back
into the sea.

■ *Above:* Waffen-SS
troops prepare for
battle as the
Normandy campaign
begins to reach its
climax.

■ *Left:* Tiger II
tanks of the army's
503rd Heavy Panzer
Battalion arrived at
the Normandy Front
in mid-July.

during a conference with Hitler, demanded that a number of *Das Reich* officers be punished. The main culprit during the massacre, SS-Sturmbannführer Otto Dickmann, was later killed in action in Normandy, and after his death the Waffen-SS leadership was able to quickly hush up the incident.

Eventually 21 rank-and-file soldiers were put on trial by the French after the war, but it was soon revealed that these men had merely been conscripts from the French-speaking Alsace region, and consequently they were able to persuade the court that they were unwilling participants. After the war, the French did not rebuild the town, and it stands today as a monument to the suffering of the French victims who died there in 1944.

One week into the invasion, the Germans seemed to be losing the reinforcement race. That was, until mother nature came to Rommel's assistance on 19 June. From that date, four days of storms raged in the Channel, with the result that two of the Allied prefabricated Mulberry harbours were smashed and some 700 ships were run ashore. The arrival of Allied reinforcements dropped to barely a trickle. Only some 9000 men a day were coming ashore and 142,247 tonnes (140,000 tons) of supplies were stranded, backed up in various depots throughout England.

Montgomery's plan for Operation Epsom had to be put back until the last week of June. During Hitler's only ever visit to the Normandy front on 17 June, he ordered Rommel to prepare a massive counterattack. This would involve six panzer divisions, which would be tasked with smashing the Allied bridgehead. Until four of these divisions arrived in the last week of June, all the "Desert Fox" could do was hang on. Whichever side struck first would have a decisive advantage.

■ *Above:* Many German units in Normandy relied on captured vehicles, such as the H39 self-propelled 105mm howitzer based on a Hotchkiss chassis, to augment their firepower.

Montgomery was first off the mark, launching Operation Epsom on 25 June. This was aimed at punching through the forward positions of the *Hitlerjugend* Division. Lieutenant-General Sir Richard O'Connor's VIII Corps commanded the offensive, while the 49th, 15th and 43rd Infantry Divisions were responsible for taking the lead in the advance.

The 11th Armoured Division was held in reserve close behind the front, ready go into action once crossings over the Odon River had been seized. Its objective was Hill 112, which dominated a swathe of the Norman countryside to the west of Caen. The gentle slopes of the hill were covered in open cornfields that provided superb fields of fire for the German gunners who were engaged in defending it. Meyer, Dietrich and Rommel correctly judged that whoever held the hill would control Caen, and with it Normandy, and they all resolved that no effort would be spared keeping it.

The British attack was sequenced, with the 146th and 147th Infantry Brigades hitting Wilhelm Mohnke's 26th Panzergrenadier Regiment at 05:00 hours. Heavy

> *The 901st Panzergrenadiers broke under the pressure and were relieved by the* Hitlerjugend *panzers*

fog covered the battlefield, making it impossible for the German defenders to strike the British infantry before they were almost on top of their positions.

Heavy fighting surged around the village of Fontenay-le-Pesnel and the nearby Tessel woods. Two companies of Panzer IVs were called up to lead a counterattack, which stabilized the situation. However, the neighbouring 901st Panzergrenadier Regiment broke under the pressure, and had to be relieved by the panzers of the *Hitlerjugend* Division By nightfall Fontenay village itself was still being fought over, with Waffen-SS men holding out in a string of strongpoints. The *Hitlerjugend* panzers, however, still managed to hold the high ground near the village of Rauray, and this vantage point was to play a crucial part in the forthcoming battle.

During the night, the commander of the *Hitlerjugend*'s Panzer Regiment, Max Wünsche, was ordered to form a Kampfgruppe to throw back the 49th Division's penetration into Fontenay. Just as the *Hitlerjugend* Panzer IVs and Panthers were advancing into the dawn, British

Shermans of the 24th Lancers and 4th/7th Dragoon Guards were also starting to roll forward into the attack from the eastern edge of the village. A fierce tank battle was developing in the fields south of the village when Meyer, who was watching from Rauray with Wünsche, started to receive reports that a major British attack was developing against the division's centre. He immediately called off the panzer attack and began moving troops to counter the new threat.

It was now the turn of the 15th Highland Division to attack. At exactly 07:30 hours, 700 guns started blasting the positions of the *Hitlerjugend* pioneer battalion around the village of St Manvieu. For 10 minutes this storm of destruction laid waste fields, villages and woods. Then the barrage started to move forward at a rate of 100m (9144yd) every three minutes. Behind this torrent of fury came two brigades of British infantry, walking with fixed bayonets. This neatly scheduled attack soon broke down into chaos when nine British Shermans exploded in a minefield laid by the pioneers. Nevertheless, despite furious resistance from the pioneers, they were just overwhelmed.

By late morning the British had pushed 3km (1.8 miles) through the *Hitlerjugend* lines, and had captured Cheux. This success was far from easily won: the assaulting regiments had each lost more than 100 men. Several British tanks were victims of Panzerfaust fire in these actions, but nonetheless it seemed that the British armour had opened a way through to the Odon. Three armoured regiments were able to cruise on forward.

However, Meyer had not finished his work yet. He ordered all of his available tanks to move to cover the breach in the line. Panzer IVs were posted in ambush positions facing eastwards on the high ground at Rauray, and Panthers moved in from their reserve positions at Carpiquet airfield in order that they might hit the British from the other flank. Both sides were poised for battle.

Dietrich now released Tigers of the 101st SS Heavy Panzer Battalion and assault guns of the 21st Panzer Division. Numbers of 88mm Flak batteries were also mustered to form an antitank gun line ahead of the British tanks. All through the afternoon and

*Behind the torrent of fury came two brigades of British infantry walking with fixed bayonets*

■ *Above:* Waffen-SS antitank units in Normandy fielded large numbers of Marder III self-propelled guns.

into the evening, the German panzer crews
and Flak gunners duelled with the British
tank crews.

As night fell, some 50 British tanks could
be seen through the darkness, burning
around Cheux. Meyer's desperate measure
had just held the line. Some panzers had
even managed to fight their way into St
Manvieu and rescue groups of pioneers
engaged in fighting behind the British lines.
German losses were grievous, though. The
*Hitlerjugend* Division lost more than 750
dead, wounded or missing, some 325 taken
from the pioneer battalion.

Montgomery and O'Connor now made
the decision to pile on the pressure even
more and ordered that the 43rd Wessex
Division be fed into the battle, allowing the
15th Division to push its 227th Highland
Brigade forward through Cheux to make a
dash for the Odon. The 4th Armoured
Brigade was brought up to roll behind the

infantry, and was awarded the responsibility
of leading the breakout.

Blocking the British axis of advance
between Grainville-sur-Odon and Marcelet
was a Kampfgruppe made up of 30 Panzer
IVs and a number of StuG III assault guns.
Based around Rauray were 17 Panthers of
the *Hitlerjugend*'s 1st Panzer Battalion,
backed by a dozen 101st Battalion Tigers.
Holding the Odon were a number of 88mm
batteries. A Panther company from the 2nd
Panzer Division was also dispatched to help
Meyer hold the line. Groups of pioneers and
panzergrenadiers had turned many of the villages along the Odon into well-fortified
strongpoints, but Meyer's defence plan relied
on the long-range killing power of his many
panzer and Flak guns.

The British attack got off to a slow start
because Cheux was clogged with troops,
tanks and supply vehicles. This chaos was
not helped by the fact that the 2nd Panzer

Division's Panthers made an unauthorized attack and that its move was beaten back, with the loss of 4 out of its 17 tanks.

A weak attack in the morning by one Scottish regiment was easily defeated by the panzers covering Rauray. Early in the afternoon, a strong force of Scottish infantry of the Argylls backed by the 23rd Hussars pushed south towards the Odon. Shermans duelled with Panthers, Tigers and Panzer IVs all through the day.

The *Hitlerjugend*'s weak infantry strength meant that it was not able to establish a continuous front along the wooded river valley, which allowed the Argylls to find an undefended route to a bridge. Just after 22:00 hours, the first tanks of the 23rd Hussars were across the Odon and fanning out towards Hill 112. Meyer heard that his vital ground was under threat when his radio interception unit picked up triumphant radio conversations from the British tanks as they advanced, apparently unopposed, from the Argylls' bridgehead at Mandrainville. Overnight the British 159th Brigade joined the Argylls, and elements of the 29th Armoured Brigade were also across the Odon, accompanied by more than 150 Sherman tanks.

## Holding Hill 112

During the night, Meyer had resorted to desperate measures to rush reinforcements to hold Hill 112. The strongpoints at Rauray and Marcelet were abandoned to release a company of Panzer IVs and panzergrenadiers, as well as an 88mm battery from the Luftwaffe. They reached the summit

■ *Below:* Churchill tanks of the 7th Royal Tank Regiment were in the forefront of Operation Epsom, supporting British infantry as they cleared Normandy villages of *Hitlerjugend* panzergrenadiers.

■ *Above:* Operation Epsom was not a success, largely due to the fanatical resistance offered by the Waffen-SS panzer divisions.

during the night and were ready and waiting when the British tanks began moving forward at dawn on 28 June. British tanks were soon burning on the slopes of the hill. However, in response, RAF Typhoon strike aircraft were called in to rocket the German tanks, enabling the British infantry to start edging forward, gradually outflanking the outnumbered panzergrenadiers. By noon the Germans had been pushed off the exposed summit of the hill.

Wünsche was soon on the scene and set about mustering the remains of his panzer regiment to contain the British breakthrough. Panthers and Panzer IVs were positioned around three sides of the hill in order to pen in the British, who were threatening to overwhelm the thinly stretched defences. The presence of 30 *Hitlerjugend* panzers, backed by 88mm Flak guns and Nebelwerfer rockets, was just enough to hold the line. Three times during the day Wünsche led his tanks forward into a storm of 17-pounder fire from the now dug-in British antitank guns in the woods along the banks of the Odon.

*The* Hitlerjugend *had been in action for 48 hours straight and was falling asleep in its trenches*

The British were still determined to hold Hill 112 whatever the cost, feeding new armoured regiments into the battle until their point units ran out of ammunition or tanks. By the time the last of Wünsche's attacks went in at 17:00 hours, some 40 Shermans were smashed on the slopes of the vital ground. As darkness fell over the battlefield, the British troops had retained their precarious foothold on Hill 112.

Meyer's division was now almost split in two by the huge British penetration. Mohnke's panzergrenadier regiment was just about holding out on the eastern edge of the British salient, and the remainder of the division was stopping O'Connor's tanks from driving directly into Caen from the east. The British were desperate to expand their breach and relentlessly attacked the *Hitlerjugend* positions during 28 June. The *Hitlerjugend* troops had been in action for almost 48 hours straight and were exhausted. Those who were not dead or wounded were falling asleep in their trenches and tank turrets. Help was now desperately needed if the division's front was not to collapse under the pressure.

Just in time, elements of the *Leibstandarte* and *Das Reich* Divisions were approaching the battlefield. They were to be launched in a coordinated attack to pinch off the top of the British salient. Kampfgruppe *Weidinger* from *Das Reich's Der Führer* Panzergrenadier Regiment was thrown in to bolster Mohnke's hard-pressed regiment around Grainville-sur-Odon. With only a handful of army Panthers in support, all Mohnke's Waffen-SS men could do was doggedly hold on to the string of villages along the north bank of the Odon through the day against attacks by a British infantry brigade with strong Churchill tank support.

### The *Leibstandarte*'s attack

On the other side of the salient, which had now been dubbed the "Scottish Corridor", two panz-ergrenadier battalions of the *Leibstandarte* entered the battle in a dawn attack from the village of Verson. Dietrich pulled together strong panzer support in the shape of 22 Panzer IVs from the 21st Panzer Division, a company of *Hitlerjugend* Panthers, and three Tigers of the 101st SS Battalion. At first the *Leibstandarte* Kampfgruppe swept all before it, sending the Monmouthshire Regiment reeling back in disorder and destroying three British tanks. The advance continued for another 3km (1.9 miles) until the British defence solid-ified around Colleville. Then tanks of the British 4th Armoured Brigade were thrown in against the *Leibstandarte*'s flank. In the face of this onslaught and a massive supporting artillery barrage, the German attack faltered. Five Panthers were lost and several other tanks damaged. The *Leibstandarte* spearhead was less than 3km (1.9 miles) from the *Das Reich* troopers in Grainville-sur-Odon. Nevertheless, the Scottish Corridor remained open to Hill 112.

During the morning of 28 June, the German command in Normandy was thrown into crisis by the suicide of Colonel-General Friedrich Dollman, commander of the Seventh Army. Dollman was the senior German officer on the Normandy Front in the absence of Rommel and Rundstedt, who had been summoned to Berchtesgaden for a conference with the Führer.

### Dollman's cyanide

The British seizure of the bridgehead over the Odon had thrown all the German plans for a counterattack against the British bridgehead into chaos. This attack was planned for 29 June with II SS Panzer Corps, which was assembling after its long road march from Paris to the southwest of Caen. At 20:10 hours, Dollman decided that the situation on the *Hitlerjugend*'s front was so precarious that Hausser's corps would have to be diverted for a immediate counter-stroke against the western flank of the British salient. Hausser replied to Dollman that his troops would not be ready to take action for another day.

Dollman was already in a precari-ous position. He had been placed under investigation by Hitler's lackeys for the loss of Cherbourg to the Americans two days before. Not wanting to face the wrath of the Führer for countermanding his attack orders, the colonel-general reached for his cyanide capsule.

The next most senior German officer in Normandy was Hausser, and within a few hours he had been ordered to replace Dollman. Fearing that it was not a good idea to change command just as his corps was about to attack, Hausser remained with his troops for one more day before handing over to SS-Gruppenführer Willi Bittrich, who was at that time the commander of the *Hohenstaufen* Division.

Throughout the night, Hausser's men were struggling to get into position for an attack at 06:00 hours. With a combined strength of more than 30,000 men, 79 Panthers, 79 Panzer IVs and 76 StuG IIIs, II Panzer Corps was the largest German armoured formation to enter battle *en masse* during the entire Normandy campaign. The corps' Tiger battalion had yet to arrive at the front, so it was unable to offer support for the attack on 29 June.

> *A tank battle developed around Cheux, and by the end of the day 60 British tanks were burning*

■ *Above:* Troops of British VIII Corps smashed through the *Hitlerjugend's* front and raced southwards to the strategic Odon bridges.

■ *Left:* British infantry advance through the corn fields of the Odon valley at the height of the Epsom Offensive.

Alerted by their ULTRA code-breaking operation, the British were well aware of the impending counterattack. Montgomery, fearful of the 11th Armoured Division's tanks being cut off around Hill 112, decided that he would pull back the 4th and 29th Armoured Brigades from the bridgeheads south of the Odon and concentrate his tanks to beat back the German attack on the flanks of the Scottish Corridor. Operation Epsom was halted. His caution at this key moment in the battle gave the Germans a much-needed respite and allowed them to shore up their front once more.

Using his ULTRA intelligence, Montgomery now decided to unleash his artillery and airpower against II SS Panzer Corps. The *Hohenstaufen* and *Frundsberg* Divisions were caught in their assembly areas around Noyers by huge artillery barrages, then waves of RAF Typhoons swooped down to machine-gun and rocket their columns.

The *Hohenstaufen* was given the objective of Cheux, at the heart of the Scottish Corridor. An attack by 100 RAF Lancaster bombers on one of the division's assembly areas played havoc with its attack and it did not roll forward until the early afternoon. With its two panzergrenadier regiments in the lead, the division quickly secured Grainville-sur-Odon. As the Waffen-SS Panzer IVs, Panthers and StuG IIIs took the lead for the advance on Cheux they ran into the British 4th Armoured Brigade. A swirling tank battle developed around Cheux, and by the end of the day some 60 British tanks were burning in the fields. Some 30 panzers and assault guns were lost

■ *Left:* The commitment of Hausser's II SS Panzer Corps stabilized the Odon Front, but it meant that Hitler's plans for a major counterattack in Normandy had to be shelved permanently.

in this battle, which failed to produce the decisive breakthrough which its tacticians had anticipated.

At the same time, the *Leibstandarte* Kampfgruppe tried to push westwards in order to effect a link-up with the *Hohenstaufen* Division. However, the *Leibstandarte*'s attack never got beyond its start-line: the Waffen-SS troopers had been hit hard by a British armoured regiment. Although the Kampfgruppe did manage to destroy 12 tanks, later on it was forced to retreat and surrender two villages to the British 43rd Division.

■ *Below:* Hill 112 became a vicious killing ground as both sides battled to control its strategic heights.

South of the Odon River, the *Frundsberg* Division was ordered to clear the British from Hill 112 for good. A rocket barrage from 60 Nebelwerfers swept the hill prior to the attack. This time the panzers led the way and the Germans cleared a number of key villages on the southern edge of Hill 112 of British infantry, and knocked out 12 British tanks. Heavy rain lashed the battlefield during the night, but Hausser was not about to give the British any respite. More rocket fire poured down on the hill and the *Frundsberg* pressed home its attacks, assisted by *Hitlerjugend* tanks firing from the southern and eastern slopes. Shortly after dawn, *Frundsberg* and *Hitlerjugend* Panzer IVs were on the summit of Hill 112. Panzergrenadier attackers were then sent forward to mop up the last remaining British bridgeheads over the Odon.

### Aftermath

In five days of bloody fighting, Montgomery almost cracked open the German front in Normandy. Operation Epsom had nearly succeeded, yet at key moments, quick thinking and aggressive defence by Waffen-SS commanders snatched victory from the jaws of defeat. Success came with a price. The *Hitlerjugend* Division was hardest hit, suffering some 1240 casualties. *Hohenstaufen* was hit hard during the Allied air attacks on 29 June, losing 1150 men in a two-day period. *Frundsberg* was not so heavily engaged and lost 570 casualties. Casualty figures for the *Leibstandarte* and *Das Reich* Kampfgruppen are not available. In total, the five Waffen-SS divisions engaged must have lost in excess of 3500 men, compared to 4020 British losses.

While the Germans had halted the British and held their line, their casualties were grievous. Unlike the British, who replaced their losses in a matter of days, the Germans had no replacements to fill their ranks. The Russians had just started a major offensive on the Eastern Front and the Führer decreed that troops in Normandy could expect no relief. General Montgomery may have been outfought by the Waffen-SS in the course of Operation Epsom, but nonetheless he was bleeding Hitler's élite panzer force white. The likes of Rommel, Dietrich and Meyer were beginning to wonder how long their troops would be able to withstand such harsh punishment.

> *Dietrich and Meyer were wondering how long their troops could withstand such punishment*

■ *Above:* **British prisoners being escorted to the rear. The retaking of Hill 112 was a brief respite for the German front in Normandy.**

# CHAPTER 7

# FLESH AGAINST STEEL

## II SS Panzer Corps defeats Operation Market Garden.

In the first week of September 1944, Willi Bittrich's II SS Panzer Corps was ordered to move to a reorganizing and refitting area north of the Dutch town of Arnhem. The unit had been in action continuously for just over two months, and was now desperately in need of a quiet period to get itself ready for battle again.

Plans were already in train to bring Bittrich's two divisions, the *Hohenstaufen* and *Frundsberg*, back up to strength, and Arnhem seemed like a good place to begin this time-consuming task. There they would be safe from Allied attack. Lightly wounded personnel were sent to hospitals in Germany in order to recover, and those in need of training were sent on courses in specialist depots.

Remaining in the Dutch barracks which had been taken over by the Waffen-SS corps were probably no more than 6000 men, who were equipped with whatever tanks, artillery and vehicles they had managed to bring with them out of France. No longer worthy of the title "division", the *Hohenstaufen* and *Frundsberg* were dubbed divisional Kampfgruppen. It was doubtful if the whole of the corps would be able to put more than 30 tanks or assault guns into the field.

Walther Harzer's *Hohenstaufen* was then ordered to move to Germany to be rebuilt there. Before it left, it was to hand over its

■ *Left:* British paratroopers captured by the *Hohenstaufen* Panzer Division during the bitter battle for Arnhem.

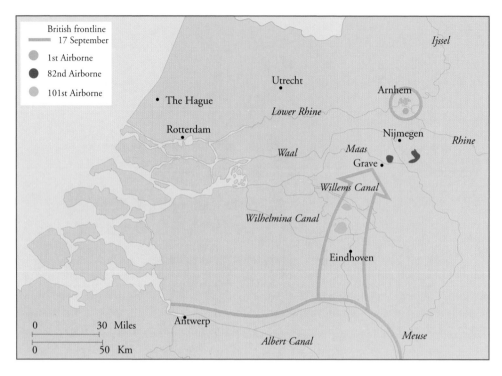

**British frontline**
— 17 September

● 1st Airborne

● 82nd Airborne

● 101st Airborne

*Ijssel*

Utrecht

Arnhem

• The Hague

*Lower Rhine*

Rotterdam

Nijmegen

*Rhine*

*Waal*

*Maas*

Grave

*Willems Canal*

*Wilhelmina Canal*

Eindhoven

0        30  Miles

Antwerp

*Meuse*

0          50  Km

*Albert Canal*

■ *Above:* Montgomery's Operation Market Garden, which aimed to finish the war by the end of 1944. The coloured shaded areas represent the drop zones for the three airborne divisions that took part. The pink circle represents Montgomery's main objective.

remaining operational vehicles and heavy weapons to Heinz Harmel's *Frundsberg*, which was to remain in Holland. At the same time as this reorganization process was under way, contingency orders were issued stating that the two units were to be prepared to dispatch "alarm" Kampfgruppen to crisis zones. Not believing intelligence reports that the Allied advance had run out of steam, Harzer decided to keep hold of many of his precious remaining tanks and heavy weapons until the very last minute, in case he had to send his men into battle. He simply ordered their tracks to be removed so they would be classed as non-operational and therefore exempt from the transfer instructions.

The conventional organization of both divisions had all but collapsed. Instead, the remaining troops were grouped into a number of *ad hoc* Kampfgruppen. Harmel gutted his panzergrenadier heavy weapons companies to form the division's only antitank gun company. Likewise, all the armoured half-tracks in the division were grouped in the

reconnaissance battalion to provide him with a powerful strike force. The artillery regiment's self-propelled gun drivers and crews were all transferred to the panzer regiment, and all the infantry were combined into three weak panzergrenadier battalions.

**Building the front at Eindhoven**

What new equipment had arrived – mainly 15 Panzerjäger IV self-propelled guns – had been dispatched to the Dutch-Belgian border, under the command of Kampfgruppe *Hienke*. This was formed around one of *Frundsberg*'s panzergrenadier battalions, an engineer and reconnaissance company. *Hohenstaufen* was ordered to provide an additional panzergrenadier battalion for this force, which was helping to build up the front south of the Dutch city of Eindhoven. It was increasingly involved in a series of inconclusive engagements along the border, and was sent into action in a futile attack against the Neerpelt bridgehead on 15 September, in which three of the Panzerjäger IVs were knocked out.

Harzer, although preoccupied with preparing to move his division by train to Germany, ordered his troops to form 19 company sized quick-reaction infantry Kampfgruppen. Much of his divisional equipment was being loaded on trains when the first Allied airborne landings occurred. His division was the closest to Arnhem itself, with the *Frundsberg* Division garrisoned farther to the north and west near Apeldoorn.

> **By September, the Allied armies in France and Belgium had largely outrun their supply lines**

Also in the Arnhem area were two other Waffen-SS units, which were not under II SS Panzer Corps command. Major Sepp Krafft commanded a Waffen-SS noncommissioned training depot to the west of Arnhem itself, and in the outskirts there was also a 600-strong battalion of Dutch Waffen-SS infantry.

Bittrich had his headquarters in a small village nearly 10km (6.2 miles) to the east of Arnhem where, in between planning the rebuilding of his corps, he would fume about how the Führer had lost the war. Once an ardent Nazi who had transferred to the Waffen-SS from the army, Bittrich was now thoroughly disillusioned with the war, and was particularly unhappy when several of his old army comrades were arrested and executed after the 20 July Bomb Plot. He, however, remained a very professional officer. His corps headquarters remained largely intact, and Bittrich had enough military pride left to ensure no one could accuse him of being unprofessional. If II SS Panzer Corps was called to fight, it would give a good account of itself.

In Arnhem's Tafelberg Hotel, Field Marshal Walther Model was trying to patch together his hopelessly undermanned and under-equipped army group to defend the northwest border of Germany. He had a reputation of being a great improviser and, after his successes on the Eastern Front, was nicknamed the "Führer's Fireman". Even at this point of the war, he was still ultra-loyal to Hitler and could still be counted on to follow the Führer's orders to the letter. He was sitting down to lunch on 17 September with his staff when hundreds of aircraft were heard flying overhead. Operation Market Garden had begun.

By the beginning of September, the Allied armies in France and Belgium had largely outrun their supply lines, which stretched all the way back to the Normandy beaches. The Germans had destroyed or still held every port on the French Atlantic coast, and the approaches to the huge Belgian port of Antwerp were still covered by German guns. With only a fraction of the needed supplies coming ashore, the Allied armies could no longer advance into Germany on a wide front. The recently promoted Field Marshal Montgomery successfully lobbied the Allied supreme commander, Eisenhower, to allow him to drive into Holland to seize bridges over the Rhine, and then turn right to advance into Germany's industrial heartland of the Ruhr.

## Multiple airdrop

The normally cautious Montgomery now came up with a very ambitious and daring plan to capture the strategic bridge across the Rhine at Arnhem with a parachute drop by the British 1st Airborne Division. The US 82nd and 101st Airborne Divisions would also be dropped to seize the bridges across the Waal and Maas rivers, as well as the Willems and Wilhelmina canals, to allow the tanks of the British XXX Corps to motor 103km (64 miles) up from Belgium to relieve the troops on Arnhem bridge. In total some 35,000 Allied paratroopers and glider-borne troops would be dropped in the largest airborne operation in military history. Lieutenant-General Brian Horrocks would predict that his XXX Corps would be in Arnhem in 60 hours.

The official history of General Eisenhower's headquarters wrote of Operation Market Garden:

"It seemed to fit the pattern of current Allied strategy. It conformed to General Arnold's recommendation for an operation some distance east of the enemy's forward positions and beyond the area where enemy

■ *Above:*
**Lieutenant-General
Brian Horrocks
(centre) was put in
charge of punching
through to relieve
the Allied airborne
divisions holding
key bridges in
Holland.**

more easterly approaches, and would carry
us to an area relatively remote from the
Ruhr.' He considered that these were over-
ridden by certain major advantages: (1) the
operation would outflank the Siegfried Line
defences; (2) it would be on the line which
the enemy would consider the least likely for
the Allies to use; and (3) the area was the one
with the easiest range for the Allied airborne
forces."

When RAF reconnaissance Spitfires pho-
tographed German tanks near Arnhem, the
deputy commander of the First Airborne
Army, Lieutenant-General Frederick "Boy"
Browning, ignored the intelligence. Other
Allied intelligence officers discounted the
idea that the remnants of II SS Panzer Corps
could put up serious resistance. The party
was on, and nothing was going to spoil the
show – except Bittrich's panzer troops.

Allied bombers and fighter-bombers hit
targets all over southern Holland during the
morning of 17 September, but the veteran
Waffen-SS men took little notice. They had
been bombed and strafed on a daily basis for
the past two months, so it had lost its novel-
ty. Harzer even went ahead with a ceremony
to present the Knight's Cross to the commander of his reconnaissance battalion, SS-
Hauptsturmführer Viktor Graebner. After
13:00 hours, when the first British paratroopers started to land to the west of
Arnhem, Bittrich swung into action, alerting
his troops with a
warning order that
was issued at 13:40
hours. With these
brief orders he set in
train the German
counteroffensive
that was to defeat Operation Market
Garden. Harzer was ordered to assemble his
Kampfgruppen and move with "absolute
speed" to contain and defeat the British airborne Oosterbeek landing. Meanwhile, the
*Frundsberg* Division was to race south and
hold the Nijmegen bridges across the Waal
to stop reinforcements reaching Arnhem.

Within minutes of receiving their orders,
Waffen-SS units sprang into action. Harzer's
men began moving into the town by whatever
means they found: trucks, tanks, halftracks,

reserves were normally located; it afforded an
opportunity for using the long-idle airborne
resources; it was in accord with Field
Marshal Montgomery's desire for a thrust
north of the Rhine while the enemy was disorganized; it would help reorient the Allied
drive in the direction 21st Army Group
thought it should go; and it appeared to
General Eisenhower to be the boldest and
best move the Allies could make at the
moment. The Supreme Commander realized
that the momentum
of the drive into
Germany was being
lost and thought
that by this action it
might be possible to
get a bridgehead
across the Rhine before the Allies were
stopped. The airborne divisions, he knew,
were in good condition and could be supported without throwing a crushing burden
on the already overstrained supply lines. At
worst, General Eisenhower thought the
operation would strengthen the 21st Army
Group in its later fight to clear the Schelde
estuary. Field Marshal Montgomery exam-
ined the objections that the proposed route
of advance 'involved the additional obstacle
of the Lower Rhine ... as compared with

> ## The Supreme Commander realized the momentum of the drive into Germany was being lost

cars, trams, even bicycles. SS-Obersturm-bannführer Ludwig Spindler, commander of the division's artillery regiment, was given command of the Kampfgruppe that would hold the western edge of Arnhem. At the same time its tank, artillery and reconnaissance units began getting the vehicles that had been deliberately put out of action to stop them being transferred to the *Frundsberg* Division into some semblance of working order. In two hours, his 400 men and 40 vehicles were rolling out of their camp towards Arnhem town centre. They had orders to move ahead of the *Frundsberg* and secure Nijmegen bridge.

On the drop zones west of Arnhem, 8000 British troops were forming up and preparing to move off to their objectives. Within minutes, Krafft's trainee NCOs were in action, fighting in the forests around the

■ *Below:* German prisoners captured by American paratroopers during their assault on Nijmegen.

**■ Above:**
**Determined and**
**quick thinking by**
**the men of II SS**
**Panzer Corps**
**thwarted Operation**
**Market Garden,**
**resulting in heavy**
**Allied losses.**

eral blocks of buildings nearby. Harmel was away in Berlin arranging for new equipment for his division, so his chief of staff, SS-Sturmbannführer Paetsch, issued orders for the units heading to Nijmegen to be diverted to an improvised ferry across the Rhine that had been established upstream from Arnhem at Pannerden. Brinkmann was told to do what he could to contain the British on the north bank of Rhine and prevent further reinforcements from reaching the bridge. He set about his task with relish.

Far to the south, Kampfgruppe *Heinke* was soon in action against XXX Corps' Guards Armoured Division as it pushed up the main road towards Eindhoven. Artillery barrages and air strikes smashed the German paratroopers defending the road, and when the Waffen-SS Panzerjäger IVs tried to help, several were knocked out. British Shermans were soon streaming northwards.

Heavy fighting now raged all around Arnhem as Harzer threw more and more troops into action to stop the British establishing a firm base. Speed of response was more important than strength or coordination. It was imperative that the British be denied the chance to establish themselves in firm positions. Spindler first threw two companies of artillerymen, fighting as infantrymen, into action during the evening of 17 September. Two bigger infantry Kampfgruppen then joined the battle. The following day, two more Kampfgruppen arrived, along with the first tanks and assault guns from the *Hohenstaufen*, as well as army units. The battle for Arnhem bridge burst into life on the morning of the 18th, when

British drop zones, delaying their advance for vital hours. One British airborne unit, the 2nd Battalion, the Parachute Regiment (2 PARA), slipped past Krafft's men and was soon marching into the town centre. Minutes before 2 PARA reached Arnhem bridge, Graebner's column raced across the huge structure and within an hour the men were in Nijmegen.

An improvised Luftwaffe and police Kampfgruppe had already secured the strategic bridge and Graebner had little to do. The *Frundsberg* Division was equally quick off the mark, and its reconnaissance battalion, under SS-Sturmbannführer Brinkmann, was on its way to Nijmegen. As the column of armoured halftracks approached Arnhem bridge, it came under fire from British paratroopers. 2 PARA now held the northern edge of the bridge and sev-

> *Graebner's column raced across Arnhem bridge and within an hour the men were in Nijmegen*

the British paratroopers heard a column of tracked armoured vehicles approaching. Graebner, being an aggressive and self-confident officer, had heard that British troops had cut him off in Nijmegen and, on his own initiative, had returned to clear the bridge for reinforcements. This was to be a *coup de main* raid to take the British by surprise and scatter them by shock action. Waffen-SS armoured halftracks, Puma armoured cars, Volkswagen jeeps and

Graebner's captured British Humber scout car raced over Arnhem bridge at 48km/h (30mph), with Waffen-SS troopers training their machine guns and rifles on the high buildings overlooking the elevated highway. Two vehicles got across the bridge unscathed and then the British Paras opened fire. Machine guns, mortars, PIAT bazookas, Sten guns and rifles raked the column. One halftrack took a direct hit and veered out of control before turning over. Other vehicles went out of control, crashing into each other and effectively blocking the road. Two vehi-cles crashed over the side of the elevated road. A handful of Waffen-SS men in the tangled wreckage tried to return fire. For almost two hours the carnage continued, until at last the remnants of Graebner's force pulled back to safety at the southern edge of the bridge, leaving 12 wrecked vehicles behind. Scores of the reconnaissance men were dead, including their commander.

## Prising out the Paras

The British Paras were not going to be removed easily. Army panzers were brought

■ *Below:* Captured Waffen-SS men are put to work by their British captors during the early phase of Market Garden.

up to reinforce Brinkmann's Kampfgruppe, and a determined effort was launched to blast out the British. As the battle was raging at Arnhem bridge, Spindler was continuing his effort to hold the 1st Airborne Division, which was pushing eastwards to help their comrades in the centre of the town. Spindler's force had grown to 1000 men in several independent Kampfgruppen, backed by 30 tanks. An *ad hoc* division of army and Waffen-SS units was also trying to build a front to block the British move westwards and to seal them in a Kessel. The Germans were closing in.

*Army and Waffen-SS units were trying to build a front to block the British move westwards*

During the morning of 18 September, Harmel returned to Arnhem and quickly received his orders from Bittrich, who declared: "Schwerpunkt (main effort) is south." No effort was to be spared to hold Nijmegen bridge and prevent a link-up between the British tanks and their airborne troops. All night his troops had been labouring to get the Pannerden ferry working and, by late morning, Waffen-SS engineers on trucks and riding bicycles at last reached Nijmegen. They immediately began preparing it for demolition. At midday, SS-Hauptsturmführer Karl Heinz Euling arrived to assume command of the bridge defence Kampfgruppe. Soon, armoured halftracks, mortars and four Panzerjäger IVs were rumbling over Nijmegen bridge. Artillery batteries were established on the north bank of the Waal to provide support.

### Laying the trap

When American paratroopers edged into Nijmegen they were met with a heavy barrage of German artillery and mortar fire, sending them scurrying back to seek cover. More *Frundsberg* reinforcements arrived during the day, and Euling's men began laying minefields and barbed wire, as well as building field fortifications. Harmel set up his command post on the north bank of the Waal, from where he could observe the key bridge. Model relayed to him the Führer's orders that the bridges were not be blown, but held to allow a German counterattack to restore the front along the Dutch–Belgian border. Harmel was having none of this nonsense, though, and was determined to order the bridge to be blown if British tanks attempted to cross. Late in the afternoon, German observation posts south of Nijmegen reported British tanks operating with the American paratroopers.

Throughout the afternoon and into the night of 18/19 September, fighting raged in Arnhem. Tiger tanks were brought up to blast the paratroopers on Arnhem bridge and the army's 280th Assault Gun Brigade arrived to support Spindler's drive against the main British force. Slowly, the Germans were becoming more organized and effective. A

■ *Below:* The British Guards Armoured Division spearheaded the drive to relieve the airborne troops trapped north of the Rhine at Arnhem. These men are members of the Irish Guards.

concerted defence line was established and the first counterattacks were launched. Losses were heavy on both sides, with most German Kampfgruppen losing 50 percent casualties. The German armour was decisive, allowing the outnumbered Waffen-SS Kampfgruppen to stand off and blast the British out of their positions.

The date 20 September signified the decisive phase in the battle. The Guards Armoured Division had linked up with the 82nd Airborne Division and planned to seize the Nijmegen bridge during the day. Harmel had some 500 Waffen-SS troopers in the town fighting alongside a similar number of Luftwaffe, army and police troops. 88mm and 37mm Flak guns were emplaced in order to protect the large road ramps leading up to the bridge, and the Panzerjäger IVs were also in the town.

### All-day bombardment

British guns bombarded the German positions throughout the day, and American paratroopers and British Grenadier Guards edged into the suburbs of Nijmegen. The

■ *Above:* Waffen-SS troops quickly built a firm defence line, trapping the British 1st Airborne Division in a small pocket at Oosterbeek, west of Arnhem town centre.

■ *Above:* A patrol from the *Hohenstaufen* Division hunts down an isolated group of British paratroopers in the suburbs of Arnhem.

bombardment knocked out the key 88mm Flak guns that provided the main defence of the bridge approach routes. In the afternoon 40 British tanks moved up to the riverbank and started to fire smoke shells onto the far bank to the west of the bridge. A battalion of US paratroopers then raced forward with canvas assault boats and set course for the northern bank of the Waal. German mortars and 20mm Flak guns raked the boats, killing or wounding half the Americans, but they kept going through the maelstrom. Once

ashore, they scattered the few old men and boy soldiers holding the rear end of bridge. As the river assault was under way, a squadron of British tanks rushed the southern edge of the bridge. Several tanks fell to Panzerfaust fire from the Waffen-SS men. The tanks just kept moving and, within minutes, were up on the bridge, machine-gunning the *Frundsberg* engineers who were still placing demolition charges. American paratroopers followed close behind. Watching horrified from his command post,

Harmel immediately ordered the bridge to be blown. The engineer officer kept pressing the detonation switch. Nothing happened. Artillery fire had damaged the initiation cable; Nijmegen bridge was in British hands. Harmel was dismayed; the road to Arnhem seemed open, yet the Shermans just stopped. They had run out of fuel and ammunition and needed replenishment. Also, more infantry were needed to clear the villages along the single road north to Arnhem, otherwise German guns would be able to pick off the British tanks with ease.

## Dash for freedom

The vital British infantry were still stuck in Nijmegen, fighting Euling's men. During the night the Waffen-SS officer gathered 100 or so of his remaining men together and made an escape bid. As they listened to more British tanks rolling over the Nijmegen bridge, Euling led his men on the walkway underneath it to the north bank and safety. They had put up determined resistance and delayed the British at a decisive moment in the battle. The price for this success was high. More than 260 German bodies were found in the ruins of Nijmegen.

On Arnhem bridge itself, meanwhile, 2 PARA was on its last legs. Out of ammunition and with almost every soldier dead or wounded, including its commanding officer, Lieutenant-Colonel Johnny Frost, the battalion surrendered during the morning of 21 September. They had no idea XXX Corps tanks were only 17km (10.5 miles) away. Thus ended an epic battle.

Even before the remains of Graebner's vehicles had been removed from Arnhem bridge, reinforcements were on their way to

■ *Right:* German armour was brought up finally to "liquidate" the trapped British paratroopers holding Arnhem bridge.

■ *Below:* As Polish paratroopers landed on their drop zone south of Arnhem, Waffen-SS troops were waiting and inflicted heavy losses.

help Harmel block any further move north by the British armour. Four StuG IIIs and 16 Panzer IVs of *Frundsberg*'s Panzer Regiment had been ferried across the Rhine on 20 September and, by the early hours of the following morning, had set up a "stop line" north of Nijmegen. The whole of the "island" between Arnhem and Nijmegen was low-lying marsh or prone to flooding. Any kind of movement off roads was impossible for tanks or wheeled vehicles, and very difficult for infantrymen. Harmel skilfully placed his forces to dominate the road from Nijmegen to Arnhem. British fears about being picked off on the raised road by German antitank fire were found to be fully justified when the Guards Armoured began advancing at 11:00 hours. When the first

■ *Right:* The Waffen-SS successfully blocked the highway between Arnhem and Nijmegen, and thus doomed 2 PARA.

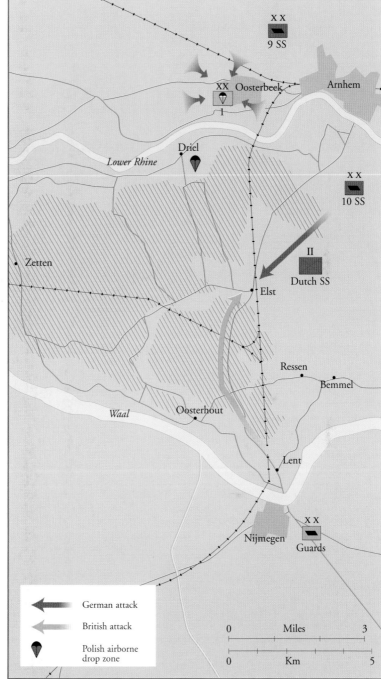

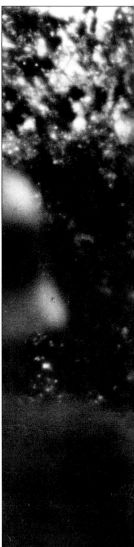

Irish Guards Sherman reached the outskirts of the village of Elst, a high-velocity 75mm round blew the tank's tracks off. More guns opened fire and four tanks were soon blazing on the road, which was now blocked. British infantry tried to attack across the open fields but were soon pinned down by Harmel's artillery. At midday on 21 September, eight Panther tanks led columns of *Frundsberg* panzergrenadiers across Arnhem bridge and moved to join Harmel's depleted Kampfgruppe north of Nijmegen bridge. With the arrival of these reinforcements, any chance the Allies had of reaching Arnhem was doomed.

## Out of Arnhem

Harzer's troops continued to press back the eastern flank of the British force east of Arnhem. He ordered his Kampfgruppe to form small penetration teams, each led by a couple of StuG IIIs, to push forward into the British lines. In addition, more guns were brought up to blast the British.

South of the Rhine, a brigade of Polish paratroopers was dropped just behind the *Frundsberg*'s "stop line". With customary promptness, Harmel reorganized his small Kampfgruppen to contain the new landing. A battalion of sailors was thrown in to hold the Poles and 16 88mm Flak guns were positioned to cover the road from Nijmegen. Batteries of Nebelwerfers were brought up to stop the Poles massing for infantry attacks. Every attempt to break through his line was rebuffed with heavy losses.

The Germans were not content just to block the Allied advance south of Arnhem. XXX Corps relied on supplies coming up the single road from Belgium to ensure it could keep pushing north. Model was determined to cut this road, which was known as the "corridor". The Waffen-SS Kampfgruppe that had been brushed aside in the first XXX Corps attack south of Eindhoven had been re-equipped and reorganized by 22 September. Its Panzerjäger IVs led a major attack on the corridor at Veghel that briefly cut XXX Corps' lifeline. American paratroopers counterattacked, driving them off, but for several hours the corridor was closed. II SS Panzer Corps had more valuable time to beef up its "stop line" south of Arnhem.

## King Tigers for Bittrich

The 1st Airborne Division continued to hold out in the face of continuous German attacks. During the night of 23/24 September, 45 army King Tiger tanks arrived to help Bittrich. He sent 30 south to help Harmel stop the Guards Armoured Division, and the rest turned westwards towards the Oosterbeek Kessel. There they were used to blast British strongpoints with spectacular effect. Determined groups of paratroopers, however, managed to knock some out with

■ *Below:* Vicious street fighting raged as the British 1st Airborne Division tried to hold onto to its precarious bridgehead north of the Rhine.

their PIAT bazookas at almost point-blank range. By 25 September, some 110 German guns were ringing Oosterbeek, bombarding the British trenches. RAF transport planes that tried to drop supplies to the beleaguered garrison had to fly through a wall of heavy Flak fire. Many of the supplies that were dropped ended up in the hands of Bittrich's men because they had captured the British drop zones.

A "final attack" was ordered by Bittrich for 25 September. Four *Hohenstaufen* Kampfgruppen made good progress, thanks to heavy King Tiger support, and one unit broke through the now depleted defences and overran a British artillery battery. Realizing that his 1st Airborne Division was on its last legs, Montgomery authorized its withdrawal during the night. After swimming across the Rhine to a precarious bridgehead held by the Poles, by dawn just under 2500 men had escaped. Bittrich's men advanced cautiously through the ruins of the Oosterbeek Kessel. They rounded up some 6000 prisoners, the majority of whom were wounded, and buried more than 1000 dead

■ *Below:* A dead Waffen-SS pioneer during the operation to wire Nijmegen bridge for demolition. The *Frundsberg*'s battle to hold up the British armour here effectively sealed the fate of the paratroopers trapped in Arnhem.

■ *Left:* Waffen-SS soldiers captured at Arnhem. The British were very impressed by the fighting qualities of their German counterparts.

British soldiers. The Americans lost another 3000 men and XXX Corps lost 1500 men, as well as 70 tanks. Bittrich's men were in awe of the fighting qualities of their British opponents, and the formalities of the Geneva Convention were generally observed during the battle. There were no accusations of the premeditated killing of prisoners that had sullied the reputation of Waffen-SS units in Normandy and later in the Ardennes,

The German losses were equally heavy. Some 8000 German casualties were recorded for all the units engaged during Market Garden, from Eindhoven to Arnhem. In the Arnhem area, more than 3000 casualties were inflicted on German units and 1725 of these were dead. The majority of these casualties were incurred by Bittrich's units.

Bittrich's men, however, had defeated Montgomery's daring bid to end the war by Christmas 1944. The prompt reaction of the Waffen-SS panzer corps had ensured the key bridge at Nijmegen was defended and then the road to Arnhem blocked. This was the vital ground of Market Garden. Bittrich had spotted this in his orders which were issued within minutes of the first Allied paratroops landing. For the next week, he ensured his Schwerpunkt remained firmly in German hands. No matter how bravely the British

paratroopers fought in Arnhem, they were doomed as soon as Harmel's Kampfgruppe took up defensive positions on Nijmegen bridge on 18 September.

Senior British intelligence officer Brian Urquhart had this to say of Arnhem: "My job as chief intelligence officer was to try to evaluate what the enemy reactions were going to be and how our troops ought to deal with them. The British airborne troops were going to be dropped at the far end of the operation at Arnhem – it was across the third bridge, so there were three bridges that had to be captured before you got to the British airborne troops. I became increasingly alarmed, first of all at the German preparations, because there were intelligence reports that there were two SS panzer divisions right next to where the British troops were to be dropped. These were the star troops of the German Army, the 10th and the 9th SS Panzer Divisions. They had been very badly mauled in Normandy and were refitting in this area. These were the best fighting troops in the German Army and they had heavy tanks. Airborne troops in those days had absolutely nothing.... They had limited supplies of ammunition, and they could not fight heavy armour because they didn't have the weapons to do it."

# CHAPTER 8

# INTO THE ARDENNES

## Hitler's last great offensive in the West in December 1944.

Field Marshal Gerd von Rundstedt announced the following to his men in the West on the evening of 15 December 1944: "Soldiers of the West Front! Your great hour has arrived. Large attacking armies have started against the Anglo-Americans. I do not have to tell you anything more than that. You feel it yourself. WE GAMBLE EVERYTHING. You carry with you the holy obligation to give everything to achieve things beyond human possibilities for our Fatherland and our Führer!"

This stirring message was read to his attack troops as they moved up to their start-lines in the heavily wooded Eifel region of Germany. At 05:30 hours the following day, 1600 German guns and rocket launchers drenched the American frontline in deadly shrapnel. Then the first attack waves of infantry moved forward to clear a route for the panzer columns, who were to be unleashed to capture their first objective – the bridges across the Meuse – within 48 hours. The panzers would push on to Antwerp and victory.

"Sepp" Dietrich's Sixth Panzer Army was placed on the right flank of the assault and it would be the Schwerpunkt, or main effort, for the attack. I SS Panzer Corps would lead the advance to the Meuse, with II SS Panzer Corps following close behind. Once the vital river crossings were secure, Bittrich's divisions would spearhead the advance on Antwerp. To help Dietrich reach the bridges before the Americans had time to destroy them, Otto Skorzeny's special forces brigade – with small teams wearing US uniforms taking the

■ *Left: Leibstandarte* panzergrenadiers sweep through abandoned US Army vehicles in the opening of Operation Autumn Mist.

■ *Below:* The US Army's 14th Cavalry Group provided easy pickings for the *Leibstandarte*, which had smashed into the northern flank of the American defences.

lead – was to race ahead of the Waffen-SS panzers and capture them in a *coup de main* operation. A regiment of Luftwaffe paratroopers was also to be dropped ahead of Dietrich's corps to capture a key road junction.

The sister *Leibstandarte* and *Hitlerjugend* Divisions would advance side-by-side towards the Meuse, after army Volksgrenadier divisions had cleared a way through the string of weak American units holding the front along the Belgian–German border. Once unleashed, the two divisions would race through the narrow forested valleys of the Ardennes until they reached the

open countryside in the Meuse valley. The region's roads were winding and poorly maintained and, in most places, could barely take single-file traffic. The constricted road network in the Ardennes meant Dietrich's divisions had to be split up into self-contained columns, each of which was assigned its own specific route, or Rollbahn. All told, more than 6000 Waffen-SS vehicles had to be squeezed through the Ardennes road system. The speed of the Waffen-SS advance was determined as much by the commanders' traffic-control abilities as their tactical skills.

The *Leibstandarte* Division was divided into three large Kampfgruppen, centred on the panzer regiment and its two panzergrenadier regiments, and a "fast group" based on the division's reconnaissance battalion. *Hitlerjugend* was organized in the same way. The most powerful Kampfgruppe was Jochen Peiper's, which had all the *Leibstandarte*'s tanks, its King Tigers, a panzergrenadier battalion carried in armoured halftracks, and a battalion of army howitzers. All told, he had more than 5000 men, 117 tanks, 149 halftracks, 24 artillery pieces, 40 antiaircraft guns, and more than 500 other vehicles. It was the *Leibstandarte*'s lead unit and the success of the offensive would depend on its progress.

The atrocious road network meant that each division was allocated no more than two Rollbahns each, so their Kampfgruppen were lined up behind one another waiting for the lead troops to blast open a way forward. With little room for manoeuvre off-road, the lead Kampfgruppe was effectively reduced to relying on the handful of tanks it could place at its head to win through. Behind Peiper's Kampfgruppe were nose-to-tail columns of tanks and trucks.

## Traffic jams

Although the Germans had amassed more than 17 million litres (3.73 million UK gallons) of fuel to support the offensive, the jammed road network meant the troops at

■ *Above* Jochen Peiper's Kampfgruppe was boosted by the Tiger II tanks of the army's 501st Heavy Panzer Battalion for its drive westwards. Here, one of its tanks passes a column of captured GIs from the 99th Infantry Division.

the front of the convoys could not rely on refuelling tankers getting through to them. So Peiper and his colleagues in the lead Kampfgruppe were ordered to seize US petrol dumps to maintain the pace of their advance.

Hitler had wanted to launch the offensive in early November, but delays in massing the necessary troops and supplies had put it back until December. This brought with it one advantage: the fog, rain and low cloud that shrouded the Ardennes provided cover from the Allied fighter-bombers that had paralyzed German panzer columns in Normandy in the summer.

On the freezing night of 15 December, the *Leibstandarte* moved into its forward

assembly areas behind the sector of front held by the 12th Volksgrenadier and 3rd Parachute Divisions. These were units that had been decimated in Russia and Normandy, and then rapidly rebuilt with personnel from rear-echelon units. They lacked heavy equipment and trained infantry commanders. The *Hitlerjugend* was waiting a few kilometres to the north, behind the 277th Volksgrenadier Division.

## American resistance

The 12th and 3rd Divisions' attacks quickly stalled in the face of very determined, but poorly coordinated, American resistance. They were supposed to have captured the town of Losheim and its key road junction in a couple of hours, to allow Peiper's tanks to roar into action as dawn broke. Minefields held up the attack, and the two divisions were still fighting their way through American positions in the early afternoon. When a breach was opened, it was found a key bridge was blocked and a temporary one had to be built by army engineers. Furious at the delay, Peiper ordered his own Waffen-SS engineers to begin building their own. It was not until well after dark that his column got into Losheim, where Peiper was dismayed to find the commander of the lead parachute regiment had allowed his men to go to sleep, rather than press on with the advance. The determined Waffen-SS officer "took" the paratroopers under his command and they were soon loaded onto the back of his King

Tigers which pressed on into the night. Several tanks and vehicles were lost when the column ran into a minefield, but Peiper ordered the advance to continue regardless.

## Peiper's column presses on

All night Peiper's men forged on, with two Panthers leading the way until they surprised an American scout company parked up in a village just before dawn. Most of the GIs were captured and subsequently filmed by Nazi propaganda teams accompanying Peiper's column. The weather briefly cleared to allow some American fighters to attack, but they were unable to inflict much damage or delay the column. Running short of fuel, Peiper now made a diversion to raid a large US fuel dump. His tanks were soon being refuelled

■ *Below:* Battle-hardened Waffen-SS troopers cautiously move past vehicles abandoned by the poorly motivated GIs holding the line in the Ardennes.

■ *Right:* The
Germans achieved
total surprise, but
the going was
painfully slow, and
soon the lead
elements were
behind schedule.

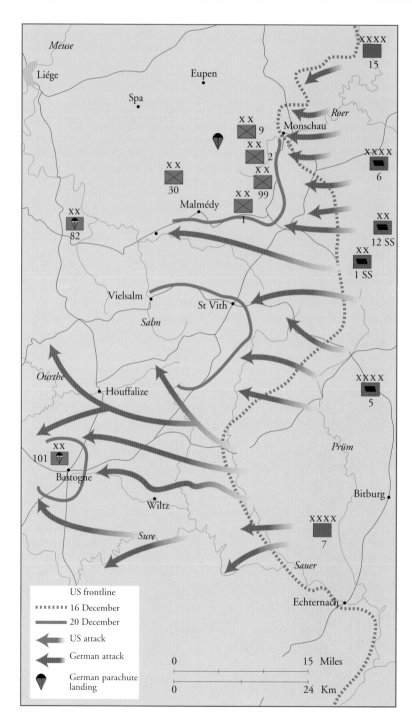

by sullen American prisoners. The Germans turned north towards the town of Malmédy.

When the lead Panzer IVs approached a crossroads in the hamlet of Baugnez they spotted a column of US soft-skinned vehicles ahead of them. They immediately started firing on the Americans, then raced at full speed towards them. Panzergrenadiers in armoured halftracks were close behind. Outgunned, the Americans offered no resistance and, in a few minutes, Waffen-SS men had herded almost 100 stunned Americans into a nearby field. Peiper then passed by in his armoured command halftrack and ordered the advance to continue, racing off westwards with his lead tanks. Learning that a US artillery brigade had its headquarters nearby, Peiper set off to capture it and its general. The American general escaped with a few minutes to spare before Peiper's tanks burst into his compound. Back at Baugnez, the captured Americans were being machine-gunned by Peiper's men in an incident that would become notorious as the "Malmédy Massacre", even though it occurred several kilometres outside the town. Peiper and more than 70 other members of the *Leibstandarte* would later face war crimes charges for their involvement in this horrific incident.

## Stopping at Stavelot

Peiper continued to drive his men forward. They kept going even after it grew dark. The Waffen-SS column was unopposed until it approached the village of Stavelot, where the lead panzers were fired upon by a single bazooka rocket. Fearing a tank ambush in the night, the Kampfgruppe pulled back to wait for daylight, not knowing that the village and its strategic bridge was held by only a few dozen Americans.

Behind Jochen Peiper's spearhead, the *Leibstandarte*'s other Kampfgruppe, led by

■ *Below:* A Waffen-SS panzergrenadier looks over the remnants of an abandoned US column in the Ardennes.

SS-Standartenführer Max Hansen, had already managed to break free and was advancing westwards. Containing the bulk of a panzer-grenadier regiment and most of the division's Panzerjäger IVs, it was operating slightly to the south of Peiper on a parallel Rollbahn.

## The Eisenborn ridge

The *Hitlerjugend* Division was not faring so well in its attempt to open up the northern Rollbahn and seize the strategic Eisenborn ridge. The US 99th Infantry Division put up stiff resistance and held the attacks by the 326th Volksgrenadier Division. Rather than being used to exploit a breach in the American line, the division's two lead Kampfgruppen had to be committed to the assault action. Although the Waffen-SS

Panthers inflicted heavy losses on the few American tanks barring their way, soon GIs with bazookas were picking off the German tanks at an alarming rate. This fierce fighting in a string of border villages allowed time for the Americans to form a firing line with their Shermans, M10 and M18 tank destroyers, and 105mm howitzers in the antitank role.

When the *Hitlerjugend*'s Panthers rolled forward on the morning of 18 December, they ran into a hail of well-aimed antitank fire. They made it to the American lines but soon 15 Panthers, 1 Panzer IV and 2 Panzerjäger IVs were ablaze. A retreat was ordered before more of the *Hitlerjugend*'s valuable armour was lost. Kraas and Dietrich ordered a rethink, and the division's Schwerpunkt was now shifted south in order

■ *Below:* The surrounded defenders of Bastogne had to rely on parachute drops to keep fighting until George Patton's armour broke through on 26 December 1944.

to try to bypass the strong defence on Eisenborn ridge. More fanatical American resistance was encountered, and the division spent four days trying to batter its way through. Dietrich concentrated four corps artillery regiments to support a large attack on 21 December, but the Americans were fighting stubbornly and were not to be moved. When the panzer regiment attacked, it lost 11 more tanks. A further attack on the following day met a similar fate, and the division was pulled out of the line to be re-assigned to push through behind the *Leibstandarte* Division.

### The last push for victory

The stalling of the *Hitlerjugend*'s attacks on the morning of 18 December meant that Peiper's Kampfgruppe was now I SS Panzer Corps' Schwerpunkt. Even so, he was still 30km (18.6 miles) from the Meuse and 48 hours behind schedule. This was not a time to worry about his flanks. Peiper pushed all his tanks forward for one last, desperate lunge for victory.

At dawn that day, Peiper renewed his attack with added vigour. The Panthers rolled at full speed into Stavelot to seize its key bridge. The now reinforced defenders knocked out the lead Panther, and Peiper – along with the lead panzergrenadiers – took cover at the edge of the village.

Grabbing a Panzerfaust, Peiper set off to take out the offending antitank gun. Another Panther arrived and destroyed the 76mm antitank gun before driving over the bridge in a hail of bullets and shells. Their position unhinged, the Americans now withdrew to safety. This action left Peiper now in control of the vital bridge.

With time critical, Peiper pressed on to seize his next objectives, the bridge over the River Amblève at Trois Ponts, and another bridge slightly farther south across the River Salm. The bulk of the Kampfgruppe headed for Trois Ponts and a small contingent was sent to the Salm. American engineers were hard at work in Trois Ponts, laying demolition charges on the key bridge and mines on

the roads as Peiper's lead Panthers rolled into town just before 11:00 hours.

A well-placed antitank gun immobilized the lead tank and, as the following Waffen-SS tank manoeuvred around the wreckage, the GIs pressed the plunger on their demolition charges. The vital bridge disappeared in a massive mushroom cloud. The same thing happened to the assault team sent to capture the Salm bridge, leaving Peiper's route on the main road westwards blocked. He therefore turned his troops around, and sent them northwards on a side road, which led through the village of La Gleize, in order to bypass the downed bridges.

Two hours later, his Panthers were through the village and heading westwards to the crossing at Cheneux. It was undefended and Peiper's tanks were soon across and heading westwards again. Allied fighter-bombers now swooped down, knocking out two Panthers and a dozen vehicles. The damage inflicted was minor, but the delay proved fatal to Operation Autumn Mist. It gave a group of American engineers just the time they needed to plant demolition charges on Peiper's next target, the bridge at Habiemont. As his Panthers arrived at the bridge at 16.45 hours, the structure was blown in front of Peiper's eyes. Twice in one day his ambitions had been thwarted. He now had to turn his column around and head back to La Gleize to rethink his options. He had only 31 operational tanks: 6 Tigers, 6 Panzer IVs and 19 Panthers. Once back there, he met up with Gustav Knittel's reconnaissance battalion which had now made its way forward, along with a small convoy of fuel tankers. News also came in that American troops had recaptured Stavelot, so Knittel was ordered to retrace his steps and open up a supply route for Peiper.

After a night spent refuelling and reorganizing his tired troops, Peiper launched them into the attack again the following morning. This time he headed northwest towards Stoumont. The first elements of a US blocking force had moved into place in the village during the night, and when his tanks

> *At dawn Peiper renewed his attack. Panthers rolled at full speed into Stavelot to seize its key bridge*

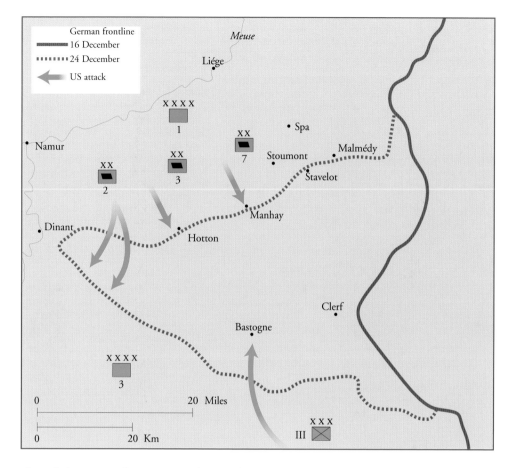

advanced, they were met by 90mm antitank gunfire. One King Tiger and four Panzer IVs were hit before German infantry cleared the village. When the advance continued, the panzers ran into a battalion of Shermans emerging out of the afternoon gloom. His route blocked, Peiper ordered the panzers back to La Gleize. With American columns closing in from four sides, Peiper was effectively trapped. He held out until the evening of 23 December, when he was given permission to break out. The details of this episode are recounted in the introduction of this book. The majority of his troops were left dead or wounded on the battlefield, along with more then 25 tanks, 50 armoured half-tracks and other vehicles. Peiper's lunge for victory had failed.

The remainder of the *Leibstandarte* Division, led by Kampfgruppe *Hansen*, was making desperate efforts to catch up with Peiper, and this soon turned into a rescue mission when the commander of the division's panzer regiment found himself cut off by American reinforcements.

### Stalled until morning
Hansen's advance had at first gone well, brushing aside a column of US reconnaissance troops near Recht on 18 December. Then it was ordered to push northwards towards Stavelot, but traffic chaos in the village prevented it moving until the morning of 19 December. Ten Tigers and Panzer IVs moved in on the village from the south, but their attack was literally stopped in its tracks

■ *Above:* By Christmas 1944, the German attack in the Ardennes had run out of steam – then the Americans counterattacked.

when an American M-10 tank destroyer hit the lead King Tiger's side armour, penetrating the monster panzer and causing it to explode. Access to the bridge was blocked. Knittel's reconnaissance unit mounted its own attack on Stavelot from the west on that day, backed by two of Peiper's King Tigers. His men reached the centre of the village but they were too late to stop American engineers blowing the bridge.

The following day, Hansen's panzergrenadiers renewed their attack on Stavelot but they now were ordered to bypass the village from the south and use forest tracks to find a route through to Peiper. The fighting in the village was some of the fiercest of the whole Ardennes campaign and a number of civilians were killed. Later, *Leibstandarte* men would stand trial for their deaths.

## Hansen by the Salm

The move westwards was more successful and soon Hansen had troops situated overlooking the Salm River. US paratroopers from the 82nd Airborne Division had now arrived in strength, and were starting to build up a strong line blocking the route through to Peiper. The rescue effort eventu-

■ *Below:* German troops loot the boots of dead GIs in a wintry Ardennes village.

ally proved futile, and all Hansen's men could do was hold open a bridgehead to receive their beleaguered colleagues. By the time Peiper's men had reached safety on Christmas Day, the *Leibstandarte* Division had shot its bolt. The destruction of Peiper's Kampfgruppe had ripped the heart out of its offensive power. It would be three days before it was able to take the offensive again.

Skorzeny's 150th Panzer Brigade fared little better than the other elements of I SS Panzer Corps. Only a handful of its sabotage teams were able to penetrate American lines, and none of them managed to seize the vital Meuse bridges. The psychological effect of their presence on the battlefield was far more important than their actual achievements. Indeed, they have entered popular legend after their exploits were immortalized in the Hollywood movie "The Battle of the Bulge". In the end, Otto Skorzeny's brigade was committed to a half-hearted frontal assault against Malmédy that was easily repulsed, giving the Americans time to destroy the town's vital bridges.

## Committing II SS Panzer Corps

Four days into Operation Autumn Mist, it was becoming clear that I SS Panzer Corps was stalled. Peiper's Kampfgruppe was stuck at La Gleize and the *Hitlerjugend* was getting nowhere on the Eisenborn ridge. It was time to commit Bittrich's II SS Panzer Corps to action. The rapid advance of Peiper created one opportunity for Dietrich. The US 7th Armored Division and parts of three other divisions were still holding out in the town of St Vith, and were preventing the Germans from securing its vital road junctions. Bittrich's mission was to push his two panzer divisions to the north and south of the St Vith salient, trapping the American force, before pushing westwards to the Meuse. It looked good on a map, but *Das Reich* and *Hohenstaufen*'s Kampfgruppen had to contend with a road network that was hopelessly overloaded. Roads were already congested with units moving to the front, supply columns and the charred remains of US vehicles. Bittrich's Blitzkrieg soon bogged down.

The *Hohenstaufen* Division led the northern pincer, pushing through Recht to attempt to seize Vielsalm. They were hoping to block this area, as it was the main escape route for American troops trapped in St Vith. SS-Sturmbannführer Eberhard Telkamp led the *Hohenstaufen*'s panzer regiment into action on 21 December, and it soon ran into a strong 7th Armored Division Combat Command, with almost 80 Shermans and tank destroyers.

## Christmas carnage

Telkamp had a Panther shot out from under him in his first clash with the Americans. Over the next two days, *Hohenstaufen* troops pressed forward time and again, only to be rebuffed. The battle came to a climax on Christmas Eve, when Telkamp ordered an all-out effort to break through to Vielsalm. Just as his panzer regiment was forming up to attack, USAAF P-47 Thunderbolt fighter-bombers swooped down in waves and massacred his column. Now the *Hohenstaufen*'s northern pincer was well and truly blocked.

*Das Reich* had been ordered south of St Vith, but its column was soon halted when the division's tankers were unable to get past road congestion and deliver the vital fuel to the vehicles. The commander of the reconnaissance battalion of *Das Reich*, SS-Sturmbannführer Ernst-August Krag, was allocated the bulk of his division's scarce fuel on 21 December for the vital task of infiltrating behind the St Vith salient to close the American escape route. The prize was to be the entrapment of 20,000 American troops. Krag's reconnaissance troopers were reinforced with a company of Panzerjäger IVs and a battalion of Wespe 105mm self-propelled guns.

■ *Left:* Once the Allies had held the German advance into the Ardennes, Waffen-SS units had quickly to form defensive lines. Here, a StuG III and 88mm Flak gun defend a road.

■ *Above:* With fuel supplies running short, large quantities of German armour and equipment had to be abandoned in the final days of the offensive.

Using back roads and tracks, Krag managed to slip through the American lines and by the evening of 23 December, he was in the village of Salmchâteau, only 3km (1.8 miles) from Vielsalm. Tanks of the 7th Armored Division were still holding the northern escape route open through that town, but Krag's appearance effectively blocked the southern route out of St Vith. His Kampfgruppe caught the last convoy out of St Vith to use this route.

In a confused night-time ambush, Krag's Panzerjägers quickly shot up the Americans' M5 light tanks, then his artillery started to rake the escaping convoy. The destruction of the American convoy was complete when Panther tanks of the army's Führer Begleit Brigade attacked it from the south. The remainder of the trapped American force had chosen to use the northern route and managed to get through to Vielsalm by

> *In a confused night-time ambush, Krag's Panzerjägers quickly shot up the Americans' M5 light tanks*

19:00 hours, and then the rearguard blew up the town's bridges.

Denied his prize at St Vith, Bittrich was now determined to push *Das Reich* forward to exploit a gap in the American defences at Manhay, which offered a route westwards to the Meuse. SS-Obersturmbannführer Otto Weidinger's *Der Führer* Panzergrenadier Regiment at last received fuel on 22 December and was launched forward with a company of Panzer IVs and StuG IIIs in the lead. It ran into a battalion-sized force of 82nd Airborne paratroopers, artillery batteries, and a platoon of Sherman tanks during the early hours of 23 December at the key Barque de Fraiture crossroads.

When the initial attack was repulsed by the Americans, Weidinger pulled back and brought up his artillery battery to soften up the defenders who were fighting in the woods around the crossroads. After several

hours spent bombarding the US position, Weidinger launched a two-pronged attack. With Panzer IVs and StuG IIIs leading the way, the Waffen-SS then closed in on the Americans. They were soon almost surrounded, then the German tanks started to pick off the Shermans and 105mm howitzers from long range. The three surviving American tanks pulled out through the last escape route, leaving the 100 paratroopers on their own amid 34 destroyed tanks and vehicles. They were soon being rounded up by the Waffen-SS men. Only 44 managed to escape in the confusion.

## Americans at Manhay

The main road to Manhay was now blocked by an American task force, so an infiltration attack was ordered to bypass its positions along narrow forest tracks westwards. Waffen-SS pioneers spent the day widening the roads to take the division's Panthers, while Lammerding's two panzergrenadier regiments were brought forward in preparation for the assault. Several fuel tankers had

also pushed through the clogged roads, so the *Das Reich* Division was set to launch a divisional-sized assault.

Setting off just after last light, the *Das Reich* columns got to within a few metres of the American positions to the southwest of Manhay when American sentries at last realized that something was wrong and started to issue challenges. At this point, it was too late. German commanders fired volleys of flares to illuminate the battlefield and then the Panthers opened fire. Within minutes, 17 Shermans were ablaze and the outlying defences of Manhay were breached. Hearing firing behind them, the bypassed American task force attempted to intervene, but well-placed Panzerjäger IVs knocked out its lead two Shermans. The task force's commander then ordered his men to take to the woods, every man for himself!

The American defenders of Manhay now realized the danger they were in and a retreat was ordered. At this point, a Waffen-SS Panther that had become lost in the night attack just outside the town took a wrong

■ *Above:* Even the mighty Tiger IIs proved unable to hold back the US advance.

■ *Above:* A Waffen-SS man captured by the US 82nd Airborne Division shows the strain of two weeks of constant fighting.

turn on a forest track and drove into the centre of Manhay. When the Americans at last realized that they had a German tank in their midst, all hell broke loose. The tank's commander, SS-Oberscharführer Ernst Barkmann, ordered his driver to reverse out of the town, as he fired off smoke grenades in order to cover their escape. Gun rounds from the Shermans and machine-gun bullets ricocheted off the Panther's armour as it made a speedy exit.

This single incident turned what had been a well-organized tactical withdrawal into a rout. Hundreds of Americans were streaming north out of the town, at the same time as the remainder of *Das Reich*'s Panthers appeared from the south. Their appearance completed the American rout, and the equivalent of a brigade of troops was now in full flight.

The following day more American tanks arrived to seal the front around *Das Reich*, backed by 18 battalions of artillery. Ordered to press on westwards, Lammerding's men soon hit a rock-solid defence. Other American tank columns began to press in

> *When the Americans at last realized that they had a German tank in their midst, all hell broke loose*

against its flanks and, two days later, *Das Reich* had to give up Manhay or face complete encirclement.

## Triple push

Three Waffen-SS divisions were now in the line, next to each other, along the northern edge of the German salient or bulge in the US front. *Das Reich* had pushed the farthest west, and next to it *Hohenstaufen* had come into line. After being rebuffed at Manhay, Bittrich was now facing two US armoured divisions. The remnants of the *Leibstandarte* were still engaged in fighting the 82nd Airborne Division between Trois Ponts and Stavelot. Fuel shortages, the terrible terrain and horrendous road congestion – coupled with heavy snow and freezing nights – were still preventing Dietrich from concentrating his army's fighting power for a decisive breakthrough. Every day that the German advance was stalled gave the Allies precious time during which to bring up reinforcements and muster their strength for their inevitable counterattack.

By 26 December, the *Hitlerjugend* Division had managed to battle its way through the grid-locked road systems and it was positioned on *Das Reich*'s western flank, ready to kick-start the stalled Sixth Panzer Army offensive. Most of the division's panzers and artillery were still stuck in jams many kilometres to the east, so the main responsibility for the attack happened to fall on the 25th SS Panzergrenadier Regiment – helped by *Das Reich*'s Kampfgruppe *Krag* – by accident rather than design.

The regiment had to attack through a heavily wooded hillside towards the village of Erezee, which was strongly defended by American paratroopers, backed by tanks. It was impossible to get any panzers or armoured halftracks through the terrible terrain, so the only fire-support available were three 75mm antitank guns that had to be manhandled by their crews up the hillside. The only other defence against American tanks were the Panzerfaust rockets carried by every man in the Kampfgruppe.

Starting out early in the evening, the heavily loaded panzergrenadiers had to march through deep snow. It took them five hours to close on their objectives. One battalion stormed into the village of Sadzot, completely surprising its American defenders there, many of whom were trying to keep warm in farmhouses rather than stand outside on sentry duty. The panzergrenadiers soon cleared the village and took many of the defenders prisoner. Surprise was not complete, though, and the Americans managed to get off a radio message calling for help before their command post was overrun. Another panzergrenadier unit pushed on past Sadzot and moved towards Erezee.

### The lost village

Kampfgruppe *Krag* had tried to advance along the main road to Erezee, via the village of Amonines. It ran into a strong road-block and lost a number of armoured vehicles in the dark, so its commander decided that it should turn back.

The Americans now launched their reserve battalion to retake the lost village. They were backed by several M5 Stuart tanks, and for several hours the US paratroopers and Waffen-SS men fought it out in the streets and houses of Sadzot. By dawn 40 dead Germans were left in the village and the panzergrenadier battalion had pulled back to the woods on its outskirts.

The 75mm antitank guns were now duelling with the American tanks, but the heavy US artillery support kept the Germans pinned down. A stalemate reigned throughout the day, during which the *Hitlerjugend* began preparations to push forward again during the course of the coming night.

After leaving behind their vehicles, Kampfgruppe *Krag* was to push forward through the forests to the south of Sadzot, leading two battalions of the 26th SS Panzergrenadier Regiment that had moved up into the line earlier in the day. Their advance was unopposed until they reached the far side of the forest, when heavy American small-arms fire stalled the attack.

■ *Above:* Captured members of Skorzeny's undercover unit were executed by US firing squads for wearing GI uniforms during the Ardennes Offensive.

A counterattack against the 25th Regiment was rebuffed and incurred heavy losses during the morning of 29 December. Those losses included the destruction of five Stuart light tanks. In terms of manpower during these clashes, more than 120 US paratroopers were lost, either killed or wounded. But such small successes were of little use.

The German High Command ordered the *Hitlerjugend* Division to halt its offensive operations during the afternoon and the division was instructed to pull back. This was not so that it could rest and recuperate: it was now to concentrate for a new offensive elsewhere in the Ardennes.

This was the high water mark of the Waffen-SS advance on the northern wing during Operation Autumn Mist. The tide had now turned irrevocably in favour of the Americans. Adolf Hitler's massive gamble in the West had failed miserably.

The fighting in the Ardennes, however, was far from over. For three more long weeks, the Waffen-SS panzer divisions would find that they were going to have many more bitter battles to fight.

> **The tide had now turned irrevocably in favour of the Americans. Hitler's massive gamble had failed**

# CHAPTER 9

# SPRING AWAKENING

## The failure of the Sixth SS Panzer Army in Hungary.

I n his Berlin bunker in February 1945, an all-out offensive led by six Waffen-SS panzer divisions to secure Hungary's oil fields seemed very logical to Adolf Hitler. Almost to a man, however, the Führer's generals thought it was madness. Huge Soviet armies were at this time on the eastern bank of the River Oder, less than 160km (100 miles) from Berlin itself. The Third Reich's élite armoured forces were needed for the last-ditch battle to defend its capital from the Russians, or so it seemed to General Heinz Guderian, the penultimate chief of staff of the German Army. The father of Germany's panzer élite could only shrug his shoulders and pass on the lunatic orders of his Führer. Hitler was now a nervous wreck, who could only keep going with the aid of drugs prescribed by his equally insane personal doctor, Theodor Morell. The Führer was reduced to moving flags around the map table in his bunker. The flags no longer represented armies or divisions, merely ghost units with no equipment or ammunition and even less will to fight. It was as if the Führer did not want to hear the bad news that his Thousand Year Reich only had a few weeks left, before it would be erased from the map for good.

The Waffen-SS panzer divisions started concentrating in Hungary in December 1944, after a Soviet offensive had pushed deep into the country and surrounded its capital, Budapest. SS-

■ *Left:* **Some 70,000 German and Hungarian troops were trapped in Budapest in December 1944, including a contingent of Tiger II tanks of the army's Feldherrenhalle Panzergrenadier Division.**

■ *Below:* General
Heinz Guderian, the
Germany Army's
chief of staff,
thought the
Führer's Hungarian
offensive was a
fatal distraction of
scarce resources
away from the
decisive battle to
defend Germany's
capital from the
Soviets.

Obergruppenführer Karl von Pfeffer-Wildenbruch and a combined force of 70,000 German and Hungarian troops were trapped in the city. What followed was depressingly predictable: a rescue force was organized; after it fought its way to within a few kilometres of the trapped garrison, Hitler refused to allow it to break out. In the end only a few hundred men were able to escape from the city.

By Christmas Day 1944, the city was surrounded. In response, Hitler ordered IV SS Panzer Corps to be moved from Poland to spearhead the rescue mission with the *Totenkopf* and *Wiking* Divisions. SS-Obergruppenführer Herbert Gille's men spent four days on freezing trains moving down to Komorno on the River Danube. They unloaded their 100 tanks and headed east to intercept Russian spearheads advancing westwards along the south bank of the Danube. Operation Konrad got under way with a night attack on New Year's Day, which initially caught the Soviet XXXI Rifle Corps by surprise. The Waffen-SS Panthers and Panzer IVs crashed through the unprepared Russians and drove eastwards for almost 48km (30 miles), knocking out 200 enemy tanks as they did so.

## Failure before Budapest

The *Totenkopf* Division advanced directly eastwards on the left flank, along the banks of the Danube, while the *Wiking* Division moved southeastwards directly towards Budapest. When the *Totenkopf* hit a strong pak-front, it too turned southwards to join *Wiking*'s push. Lacking the strength to batter his way past Soviet defences, Gille used his veteran troops to try to dodge past Soviet strong-points and find a way through to Budapest. With the route south blocked, he sent *Wiking*'s *Westland* Panzergrenadier Regiment on a march deep behind enemy lines after it found a route over the Vertes Mountains. With the Soviets now alerted to the German intentions, though, it was not long before they moved reinforcements up to close off the northern route into the Hungarian capital.

On 12 January 1945, the Waffen-SS troops pulled back from the front and disappeared into the forests along the Danube. The Soviets were convinced they had seen off the German attack. They had no idea that Gille's troops were in fact moving south to open a new front. Six days later they burst out of the morning mist to smash into the Russian CXXXV Rifle Corps, which without tank support was an easy target for the Waffen-SS units. The German tanks rolled over its frontline positions on 18 January, and then started to shoot up its supply convoys and artillery positions. By the evening they had covered 32km (20 miles), brushing aside a counterattack by the weak Soviet VII Mechanized Corps. More Russian tanks

were sent into action the following day, and they received the same treatment. The *Totenkopf*'s antitank battalion, deployed with the advance guard of the division's *Totenkopf* Panzergrenadier Regiment, was instrumental in breaking up several counterattacks by the Soviet XVIII Tank and CXXXIII Rifle Corps. Its new Panzerjäger IVs self-propelled guns were particularly effective. This heavily armoured version of the Panzer IV tank was equipped with the powerful L/70 75mm cannon, which was also used in the Panther tank. The Danube valley, with its open fields and small villages, was ideal tank country. The winter frost meant the ground was still hard, so Gille's handful of panzers was able to race forward across country. They crossed the Szarviz Canal in a night-time assault, and by the morning of 20 January German armour was on the banks of the Danube. Gille's men now motored northwards, cutting into the rear lines of communications of the Soviet Fifty-Seventh Army. The Red Army was in a panic. The Soviet commanders on the west

bank of the Danube were convinced they would soon be surrounded by IV SS Panzer Corps and the German Army's 1st Panzer Division. On 24 January, the *Wiking* and *Totenkopf* Divisions surged forward again, inflicting heavy losses on the Soviet V Guards Cavalry and I Guards Mechanized Corps. They got to within 24km (15 miles) of Budapest before the arrival of the last Soviet reserves, XXIII Tank Corps, stopped them in their tracks. Gille's men attacked with great *élan*, and used their tried-and-tested infiltration tactics to take advantage of the weakened state of the Soviet infantry divisions around Budapest. Most Soviet infantry divisions and tank corps were reduced to less than 5000 men each, following several months of non-stop fighting through the Balkans. It appeared that victory for the Waffen-SS divisions was at hand.

Three days later, 12 Soviet infantry divisions joined the tank corps in a major counterattack against the Waffen-SS divisions. The SS units held their ground, but Hitler now ordered IV SS Panzer Corps to fall back

■ *Above:*
**Hungarian gunners try to defend their capital, Budapest, from the Soviet advance. Thousands of Hungarians defected in late 1944 as it became clear that the German cause was lost.**

so it could regroup and join a major operation he was planning to defeat the entire Soviet army group in Hungary. Ignoring pleas from his generals that now was the moment to order a break-out from Budapest, Hitler refused to consider the idea. Budapest would be relieved by the Sixth SS Panzer Army. Therefore, there was no need for a break-out.

The situation reminded many German generals of Stalingrad two years before. Pfeffer-Wildrenbruch followed his Führer's orders to the letter. Hitler decorated him with the Knight's Cross for his bravery, but some thought the Führer was just trying to shame the Waffen-SS general into not surrendering. With Gille's men now falling back in the face of massive pressure, the Budapest garrison's position was becoming even more precarious. Now free from the need to deal with rampaging Waffen-SS panzers, the Soviets were able to concentrate

■ *Right:* IV SS Panzer Corps' attempt to relieve Budapest, January–February 1945.

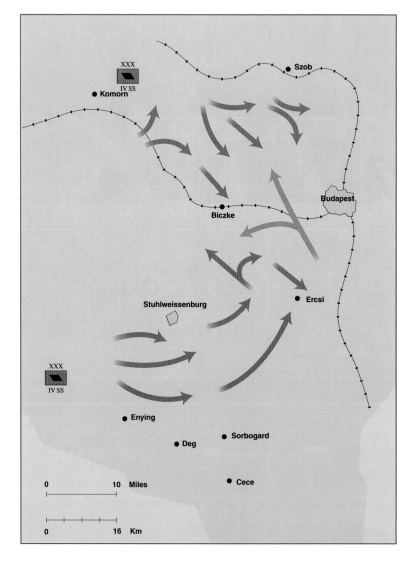

all their efforts on eliminating Pfeffer-Wildrenbruch's hapless command. The Waffen-SS general proved to be particularly inept, allowing his main supply dump to be overrun. It was only a matter of time before Budapest went the same way as Stalingrad.

In January 1945, five Waffen-SS divisions were in the process of pulling out of Belgium after the failure of the Ardennes Offensive. Hitler wanted them concentrated to lead his offensive into Hungary, which he thought would turn the course of the war. He repeatedly told his generals that they did not understand that modern warfare was about the control of economic resources. A special order was issued by the head of the SS, Heinrich Himmler, for the divisions to be pulled back into Germany to be refitted for their new offensive. Almost the total production of Germany's shattered armaments industry was to be diverted to the SS divisions. In the skies over the Third Reich, British and American bombers were pounding Germany's factories and cities on an almost daily basis, while Russian tanks were

rampaging through the Silesian industrial region. The efforts to re-equip the Waffen-SS divisions therefore stretched Germany's armaments industry to the limit. There were no more reserves left. The coming offensive would be the last throw of the dice for Hitler's Third Reich.

Throughout January and into February 1945, new tanks, assault guns, halftracks, artillery and other equipment arrived by train at barracks and training grounds in central Germany. Thousands of raw recruits and drafted Luftwaffe and Kriegsmarine (German Navy) personnel, who no longer had aircraft or ships to serve in, found themselves impressed into the Waffen-SS. Crash training courses were organized to try to mould this raw material into an élite fighting force. The results were very mixed.

For the first time, six SS panzer divisions would be committed to an operation on the Eastern Front under the command of SS panzer corps, and two of those corps would be under the command of the Sixth SS Panzer Army. This army had been raised in

■ *Above:* Waffen-SS panzer regiments made great use of StuG IIIs to augment their understrength tank companies during the final months of the war.

September 1944 to lead the Waffen-SS panzer divisions in the Ardennes. Hitler's favourite Waffen-SS general, SS-Oberst-gruppenführer Josef "Sepp" Dietrich, remained in command of this army, even though he obviously did not relish such a high-level command. He left most of the day-to-day running of the army to his staff and concentrated on what he liked doing best: carrying out morale-boosting visits to frontline regiments. Dietrich loved being in the thick of the action, and relished organizing small squads of men for daredevil operations. Not surprisingly, therefore, many army generals – and some Waffen-SS ones as well – thought Dietrich had been promoted way beyond his ability. He just about coped as a divisional commander, but was out of his depth as a corps and army commander. The Führer would not have a word said against him, however, because of Dietrich's early work as Hitler's bodyguard in the 1920s.

There was great rivalry between the two corps in the Sixth SS Panzer Army. The most favoured formation was I SS Panzer Corps *Leibstandarte Adolf Hitler* led by SS-Gruppenführer Hermann Priess, the former commander of the *Totenkopf* Division. It boasted the *Leibstandarte* and *Hitlerjugend* Divisions (the latter was to see action on the Eastern Front for the first time during the coming offensive). The *Leibstandarte* Division's panzer regiment was reinforced with a full battalion of 36 of the new super-heavy Tiger II, or King Tiger, tanks. These 71.12-tonne (70-ton) monsters boasted frontal armour 250mm (9.84in) thick that was impervious to almost all antitank weapons then in service. However, they were notoriously mechanically unreliable, and more would be abandoned on the battle-fields of Hungary following breakdowns than were lost to enemy fire. The 501st SS Heavy Panzer Battalion was one of three such units created by the Waffen-SS in the final months of the war, which used the Tiger II tank. These units grew out of the Tiger I companies that had served with the three original SS panzer divisions since 1943. The two other battalions, the 502nd and 503rd, were sent to the East Prussian and Berlin sectors in the final months of the war, and so missed the offensive in Hungary. The *Leibstandarte*'s other panzer battalion fielded 27 Panzer IV tanks, 41 Panthers and eight antiaircraft tanks. The latter were now essential to tank operations because of Allied air supremacy, which made it very risky for Germans tanks to move around in the open during daylight hours.

The *Hitlerjugend* Division could only muster one battalion for its panzer regiment, with 40 Panzer IVs and 44 Panthers. The division also had 20 of the new Jagdpanzer IV antitank self-propelled gun, plus more than 150 armoured halftracks. Also attached to the division was the 560th Heavy Anti-Tank Battalion, which fielded 31 Jagdpanzer IVs and 16 Jagdpanthers. This latter vehicle combined a Panther chassis with a fixed 88mm cannon.

A heavy punch was also packed by II SS Panzer Corps, under the command of SS-Gruppenführer Willi Bittrich, which contained the *Das Reich* and *Hohenstaufen* Divisions. Like I SS Panzer Corps, Bittrich's command had a heavy artillery regiment equipped with towed 210mm howitzers, and a rocket launcher regiment with Nebelwerfers to provide heavy fire support during assault operations.

Bittrich's panzer regiments were short of tanks, but the shortfall was made up with Sturmgeschütz (StuG) assault guns. They were distributed to the panzer regiments' second battalions to augment their Panzer IVs. The *Das Reich* Division boasted 34 Panthers, 19 Panzer IVs and 28 StuG IIIs, while the *Hohenstaufen* Division had 31 Panthers, 26 Panzer IVs and 25 StuG IIIs. The *Hohenstaufen*'s sister division, *Frundsberg*, had served in II SS Panzer Corps all through the Normandy campaign, at Arnhem and during the Ardennes Offensive, but in January 1945 it was detached and posted to the Vistula sector of the Eastern Front, taking with it its 38 Panzer IVs and 53 Panthers. It would not join the rest of the Sixth SS Panzer Army for the Hungary offensive.

Hitler was determined that the move of Dietrich's army to Hungary be kept secret,

■ *Below:* A Waffen-SS fighting patrol probes Soviet defences in the run-up to the German offensive to free Budapest.

so he ordered the famous Waffen-SS general to move his headquarters to the Eastern Front via Berlin. There he made a number of high-profile visits to the front in an attempt to convince the Soviets that the Waffen-SS panzer reserve was about to be committed to the defence of Germany's capital. The *Leibstandarte*'s King Tigers were also shipped via the Reich's capital to add to the pretence. The chaotic state of Germany's rail network at this point in the war meant the exercise was fraught with risks, and the trains carrying the tanks were lucky to have escaped the attention of Allied bombers and make it to their start line in Hungary.

Operation Spring Awakening was envisaged by Hitler as a knock-out blow against Soviet forces in the Balkans. The initial phase of the assault would be a three-pronged pincer attack to trap and destroy the Russian troops on the west bank of the River Danube. German forces would then turn eastwards and free the trapped garrison in Budapest. There was then talk of the offensive continuing southwards to drive the Red Army out of the Balkans altogether and regain control of Romania's oil wells. However, the whole scheme was based on fantasy. For one thing, Budapest was on the brink of falling even before Dietrich's troops had started their attack.

On 16 February, Pfeffer-Wildrenbruch led a breakout attempt at the head of the last 16,000 German troops in the city. They did

■ *Below:* A 150mm Hummel self-propelled howitzer. These vehicles were used to launch barrages against Soviet positions blocking the German advance on Budapest.

■ *Left:* The Jagdpanther was the ultimate German tank killer. Equipped with an 88mm cannon, sloped armour and possessing high mobility, it could out-shoot and out-fight anything in the Soviet inventory.

■ *Left:* By the spring of 1945, the Tiger I (seen here) had largely been superseded in Waffen-SS service by the more heavily armed and armoured Tiger II.

not get very far before they were ambushed. The Waffen-SS general tried to escape through the sewers, only to emerge in the middle of a Soviet regiment and was captured. Only 785 Germans made it through the Soviet ring.

As the pitiful drama in Budapest was entering its final act, Dietrich's Sixth SS Panzer Army was at last arriving in Hungary in some strength. The German offensive would be conducted in two phases. It was to kick off with a preliminary operation, code-named South Wind, by I SS Panzer Corps to destroy the Soviet bridgehead on the western bank of the River Gran, which threatened the German left flank along the banks of the Danube. The Soviet bridgehead, held by seven infantry divisions and a number of armoured units, was to be bludgeoned out of existence by a head-on attack by the *Leibstandarte* and *Hitlerjugend* Divisions.

SS-Obersturmbannführer Joachim Peiper, commanding the *Leibstandarte*'s panzer kampfgruppe, was to lead the attack, which was channelled by a series of wide water courses into a narrow 16km (10-mile)

frontage. The battlefield was criss-crossed by numerous canals, which were heavily defended by Russian antitank guns and dug-in T-34/85 tanks. The latter was the upgraded version of the famous Soviet tank, which now boasted an 85mm high-velocity cannon as its main armament. Peiper commanded all the *Leibstandarte*'s tanks, including its Tiger IIs, a battalion of panzergrenadiers riding in armoured halftracks, and a battalion of self-propelled artillery.

Army infantry units were initially committed to the battle during the evening of 16/17 February, after a corps fire mission by all the German guns facing the bridgehead. The attack achieved surprise, and the infantrymen were at first able to advance 8km (five miles) before they ran into the first enemy pak-front. Peiper ordered his King Tigers to motor to their assistance. When the heavy tanks rolled into the range of the Russian antitank guns, they started attracting heavy fire from the 76mm cannons. The shells just bounced off the front of the King Tigers, however, allowing the German tanks to destroy all the Soviet guns blocking the advance.

By evening, the *Leibstandarte* and *Hitlerjugend* Divisions were at Parizs Canal and making plans to expand the small bridgeheads they had seized. *Hitlerjugend* combat engineers built a bridge capable of bearing Panzer IV and Panther tanks, to allow them push another 16km (10 miles) into the bridgehead. During the day the Russians mounted repeated small-scale attacks against the Waffen-SS incursion, inflicting casualties and delaying the advance. Armoured kampfgruppen from both divisions advanced on 19 February, employing panzerkeil tactics. With the heavy King Tigers and Panthers in the lead, any Soviet tanks or antitank guns that tried to block the German advance were quickly silenced by the panzers' devastating firepower. By early afternoon the Waffen-SS tank crews were at the Danube, in the eastern bottom corner of the bridgehead.

The next day, the armoured spearhead was ordered to swing north to deal with the Soviet IV Guards Mechanized Corps that was still entrenched on the west bank of the Gran. Peiper decided that the attack should go in during darkness to protect the assault group of Panzer IV tanks from a huge Soviet

■ *Below:* **The effort to break through to Budapest ended in failure, and the Hungarian and German defenders of the city were left to their fate. Less than 1000 escaped to German lines.**

artillery position on the east bank of the Gran. The panzers rolled into action with flares and burning tanks illuminating the battlefield. Several German tanks were lost, but the route north was opened. The *Leibstandarte* Division now halted its tanks to refuel and rearm. The *Hitlerjugend*'s 25th Panzergrenadier Regiment was then ordered into action against the northern flank of the IV Guards Corps' bridgehead. Attacking southwards during the evening of 22/23 February, the combined panzer-infantry operation degenerated into confusion when German units failed to recognize each other in the darkness and started trading fire. This attracted Russian artillery fire, and the assault was stalled in no-man's land for several hours. Then the assault tanks got stuck in a minefield, losing several vehicles. Only a daring flank attack by the division's armoured personnel carrier battalion saved the day. By chance it found a route around the minefield, and was soon inside a village

full of T-34 tanks. The panzergrenadiers dismounted and stalked the Russian tanks though the village with Panzerschreck handheld antitank rocket launchers. With no infantry to protect them, the Russian tanks were soon fleeing from the village. This opened the way for the rest of the division to move through a path in the minefield, and clear the remaining Russian positions.

After a day recovering from this carnage, I SS Panzer Corps spent 23 February preparing for the final assault on the Soviet bridgehead. The two Waffen-SS divisions staged a concentric night attack, with King Tigers and Panthers leading the way. In only six hours of heavy fighting the position was cleared, and the Russians eventually withdrew, blowing up the last bridge across the Gran at 08:30 hours on 24 February. They left a trail of destroyed and abandoned equipment behind them. More than 2000 Russians had been killed, a further 6000 wounded and 500 captured by I SS Panzer

■ *Below:* Soviet tank-riding infantry leap into action as they move forward to mop up the last pockets of German resistance in Budapest.

Corps. Some 71 tanks and 180 artillery pieces were also lost in the week-long battle. The Waffen-SS paid a heavy price for the victory, though, losing almost 3000 casualties and a dozen tanks destroyed. Scores more tanks were badly damaged, and had to be pulled back from the panzer regiments for urgent repairs. Some of the manpower losses were replaced with more half-trained draftees from the Luftwaffe, indicating the low quality of the personnel now available to the Waffen-SS.

With the Gran bridgehead eliminated, Hitler was now able to order Operation Spring Awakening to roll forward to the south. Some 400,000 German troops, supported by 7000 artillery pieces, 965 Luftwaffe combat aircraft, and 400 tanks and self-propelled guns were to attack on 6 March. The schwerpunkt, or main effort, of the operation was between Lakes Balaton and Valencei, with the Sixth SS Panzer Army leading the way. It had the bulk of the German armour under its command. Gille's IV SS Panzer Corps was to support the operation on the left flank of Dietrich's army. For the first time ever, six Waffen-SS panzer divisions would roll forward into battle together. Not surprisingly, the Führer was very optimistic about Spring Awakening's prospects. In Hungary, though, the Waffen-SS commanders were far from optimistic about the coming battle. They were expected to advance over waterlogged terrain, which was dissected by numerous rivers and canals. Of greater concern was the fact that the Russians knew they were coming.

In the month since Gille's panzers had attacked, the approaches to Budapest were now protected by heavily dug-in antitank tank guns and infantry positions. To the south of the city, where Dietrich's attack was to be made, the Soviets based their defensive plans on the network of canals that ran across the flat plain. The start of the spring thaw also worked in the defenders' favour, because it made movement off road by any type of vehicle, even tracked ones, almost impossible. Some 16 Russian rifle divisions were in the path of Dietrich's panzers, with two tank corps and two mechanized corps, with some 150 tanks, in direct support just behind the frontline southwest of Lake Balaton itself.

■ *Above:* Soviet tank columns were held ready near Budapest, before being launched westwards along the Danube valley with the objective of capturing Vienna.

More ominously for the Third Reich, the Soviets were building up their armoured forces north of Budapest for their own offensive along the Danube valley – the Sixth SS Panzer Army would attack into the jaws of an overwhelming Soviet armada of more than 1000 tanks. The attack plan called for I SS Panzer Corps to advance southwards to link up with the Second Panzer Army advancing northwards. II SS Panzer Corps was to move directly eastwards towards the Danube, to protect the right flank of the Waffen-SS attack.

Operation Spring Awakening began officially at 04:30 hours on 6 March, with a massive barrage from the artillery of the Sixth SS Panzer Army. First to move forward were the panzergrenadiers of the *Leibstandarte*, whose first task was to open several lanes through a Russian minefield before they could begin clearing an extensive system of trenches and strong-points at bayonet point. This took all the morning, and then the division's panzer kampfgruppe was able to race forward. After a few kilometres, though, it ran into a well-prepared pakfront, protected by more minefields. As the kampfgruppe's tanks and armoured half-tracks tried to deploy off the roads to engage the enemy antitank guns, they started to get stuck in axle-deep mud. The panzergrenadiers had to press home their attacks without armoured support. Not surprisingly, the rate of advance was unimpressive.

Advancing on the *Leibstandarte*'s left, the *Hitlerjugend* Division found the going equally hard. Its tanks also got stuck in the mud, and the division was only able to push 1.6km (one mile) forward. II SS Panzer Corps' attack did not even reach its assembly area until well after dark. Thanks to their successful initial defence, the Russians were able to deploy an extra infantry corps, with limited tank support, across the path of I SS Panzer Corps. They did not move their main armoured reserves, but kept them around Budapest in preparation for their own offensive.

■ *Left:* Budapest's Royal Palace was destroyed in the heavy fighting for the city after German troops turned it into a strong-point.

On 7 March the German attack began to gather momentum, as both the *Leibstandarte* and *Hitlerjugend* Divisions at last broke through the Soviet defences and were able to launch their panzer kampfgruppen into action to exploit the breaches created by the panzergrenadiers. During the night, the Soviet infantry divisions began a deliberate withdrawal back to the Sio Canal, where a new defensive front was being prepared by the reserve divisions. II Panzer Corps' attack did not get very far before it ground to a halt in waterlogged ground. One tank even sank up to its turret ring in the mud!

As dawn broke on 8 March, German fortunes looked as if they had changed. The *Hitlerjugend* surged 16km (10 miles) forward until it ran into a pak-front dug-in on ridge lines. The division's reconnaissance battalion was ordered to take the position in a night attack, to allow the advance to begin again at first light. A dozen Jagdpanthers and Jagdpanzer IVs formed a panzerkeil which charged up the hill and routed the defenders. The reconnaissance battalion's halftracks followed close behind, and the Waffen-SS troopers machine-gunned and grenaded the fleeing Russian troops as they drove among them.

Bittrich's men, spearheaded by *Das Reich*, now ran headlong into the Soviet XXX Corps and XVIII Tank Corps, which battled furiously to hold them back from the Danube. The Russians even resorted to using their heavy antiaircraft artillery in the direct-fire mode against German tanks. The next day the *Hohenstaufen* and *Wiking* Divisions joined the attack, driving a wedge 24km (15 miles) into the Soviet line.

I SS Panzer Corps now caught up with the retreating Russians on the Sio Canal, with German Panthers and Jagdpanthers inflicting heavy losses on a number of Soviet truck convoys that had not yet crossed over the canal.

For the next two days, *Leibstandarte* and *Hitlerjugend* panzergrenadiers battled to cross the Sio Canal. Small Russian rearguard

■ *Below:* Soviet infantry trade fire with German snipers in the ruins of Budapest. The operation to capture the city, and the defeat of the Waffen-SS relief effort, left Austria and southern Germany wide open to Soviet attack.

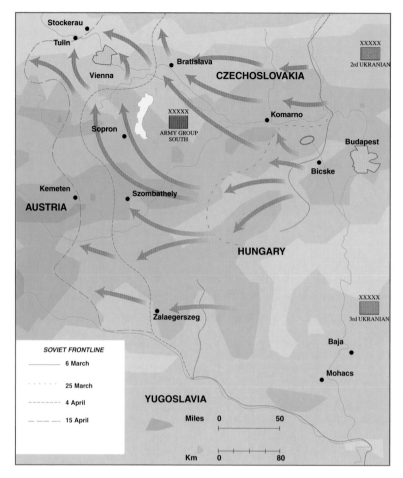

■ *Left:* Soviet offensives in Hungary, Czechoslovakia and Austria, March–April 1945.

detachments had to be evicted, one-by-one, from a series of villages on the north bank of the canal. King Tigers were brought up to deal with the Soviet antitank guns and Su-100 assault guns that were left behind to slow up the German advance. Heavy rain and sleet made this miserable work, and scores of vehicles got stuck in mud as they tried to manoeuvre through the fields along the canal bank. Soviet Stormovik fighter-bombers then appeared over the battlefield, and picked off many of the immobilized German tanks.

II SS Panzer Corps also kept battering its way forward, albeit at a snail's pace, with *Das Reich*'s panzer regiments having a good day knocking out scores of Soviet tanks. To pen in this incursion, the Soviet XXIII Tank Corps was thrown into the battle against the Waffen-SS division.

The fighting along the Sio Canal reached a climax on 12 March with a major effort being mounted to push bridgeheads across the 30m- (98.42ft-) wide obstacle. The *Hitlerjugend*'s attack ended in a slaughter, when its fire-support panzers and Jagdpanzers were forced to fall back from the canal bank by a withering barrage of antitank gun fire. The panzergrenadiers pressed on, only to be machine-gunned in their rubber assaults boats as they tried to row across the canal. A few of them made it across and established a precarious bridgehead. In the *Leibstandarte*'s sector, the attack fared better because the division was able to bring its troops forward through a town and protect them from enemy fire until the last moment, before they too rushed across the canal. Deadly 88mm flak guns were brought up to support the assault and, along with the King Tigers, they were able to neutralize many of the Soviet antitank guns and machine-gun bunkers. This firepower was enough to allow the establishment of a bridgehead during the night, and soon the division's combat engineers were at work erecting a tank bridge. A Jagdpanzer IV got over the structure, but the weight of a second vehicle was too much and it collapsed into the water. Constant repairs were needed to keep it open to allow reinforcements to cross. They were desperately needed to deal with a counterattack by a regiment of T-34/85 tanks.

I SS Panzer Corps managed to hold onto its bridgeheads for three more days in the face of incessant Soviet counterattacks. Battalions, then regiments, were fed into the battle by the Soviets to keep the Waffen-SS penned in. The Red Army was winning the battle of attrition.

*By 20 March, I SS Panzer Corps could only muster 80 tanks, assault guns and self-propelled guns*

With his route south effectively blocked, Dietrich decided on 15 March to switch the schwerpunkt of his army away from I SS Panzer Corps to Bittrich's front. The *Leibstandarte* and *Hitlerjugend* were ordered to disengage and move north, before joining the attack towards the Danube.

The following day, however, the Soviets began their own offensive, which rendered Dietrich's orders irrelevant. More than 3000 vehicles, including 600 tanks, poured past Budapest and swept around both sides of Lake Valencei. Gille's IV SS Panzer Corps was engulfed in the storm, with the *Wiking* Division all but surrounded after a Hungarian division collapsed on its flank. Hitler issued orders that the division was to hold at all costs. The division's commander, SS-Oberführer Karl Ullrich, ignored the orders and pulled his troops back before they were trapped. The *Hohenstaufen* Division came to its rescue, also in defiance of the Führer's orders.

Bittrich and Gille now joined forces to hold open an escape route for I SS Panzer Corps, which was pulling back north as fast as it could to avoid encirclement. It managed to get out of the trap, but had to leave most of its damaged and bogged-in vehicles behind. By 20 March 1945, I SS Panzer Corps could only muster 80 tanks, assault guns and self-propelled guns fit for service. The remainder of Dietrich's army now mustered fewer than 100 tanks and assault guns. All the Waffen-SS divisions had suffered grievously during Spring Awakening, and most were below 50 percent strength and there was little prospect of any reinforcements to replace losses.

The German front in Hungary was shattered wide open by the Soviet offensive. It was never re-established. Dietrich's army started to fall back to Austria in the hope of defending the capital, Vienna. The Waffen-SS divisions were now constantly retreating, though every so often a handful of tanks and panzergrenadiers would turn to form a rearguard. However, they were soon outflanked and the retreat would begin again.

When news reached Hitler's bunker about the retreat of the Waffen-SS, the Führer flew into a rage. The failure of his precious SS divisions was all the more hard to bear due to the faith he had previously had in their ability and Nazi ideological zeal. He sent a signal to Dietrich ordering the soldiers of the Sixth SS Panzer Army to remove their honourific Nazi armbands. In his eyes they were no longer fit to wear the Führer's name on their uniforms.

The effect on the morale of the Waffen-SS divisions in Austria was catastrophic. Senior commanders ripped off their medals in disgust and ordinary grenadiers started to desert in large numbers. The men of Dietrich's army could see that the war was lost. Now, therefore, the main priority was to escape to the west to surrender to the Americans, and thus avoid the inevitable retribution at the hands of the soldiers of the triumphant Red Army.

# BIBLIOGRAPHY

Badsey, Stephen, *Normandy 1944*, Opsrey, London, 1990

Bishop, Chris, *WWII: The Directory of Weapons*, Aerospace Publishing, London, 2000

Blumenson, Martin, *The Duel for France, 1944*, Da Capo Press, USA, 1963

Brett-Smith, Richard, *Hitler's Generals*, Osprey, London, 1976

Carrell, Paul, *Invasion – They're Coming!*, George Harrap, London, 1964

Cooper, Matthew and Lucas, James, *Panzer*, Macdonald, London, 1976

Cooper, Matthew and Lucas, James, *Panzergrenadier*, Macdonald and Jane's, London, 1977

Cooper, Matthew and Lucas, James, *Hitler's Elite*, Grafton, London, 1990

Delaforce, Patrick, *The Black Bull*, Chancellor Press, London, 2000

Downing, David, *The Devil's Virtuosos*, New English Library, London, 1976

Edwards, Roger, *Panzer: A Revolution in Warfare, 1939–45*, Arms and Armour, London, 1989

D'Este, Carlo, *A Genius For War*, HarperCollins, London 1996

Guderian, Heinz, *Panzer Leader*, Futura, London, 1979

Gudgin, Peter, *Armoured Firepower*, Sutton Publishing, Stroud, 1997

Forty, George, *German Tanks of World War Two*, Blandford Press, London, 1987

Hastings, Max, *Overlord*, Michael Joseph, London, 1984

Hastings, Max, *Das Reich*, Michael Joseph, London, 1981

Hitler, Adolf (trans Norman Cameron), *Hitler's Table Talk*, Weidenfeld & Nicolson, London, 1953

Irving, David, *The Trail of the Fox*, Weidenfeld & Nicolson, London, 1977

Jentz, Thomas, Doyle, Hilary and Sarson, Peter, *Tiger I*, Osprey, London, 1993

Jentz, Thomas, *Panzer Truppen*, Schiffer Military History, Atglen, 1996

Keegan, John, *Six Armies in Normandy*, Pimlico, London, 1982

Kershaw, Robert, *It Never Snows in September*, The Crowood Press, Marlborough, 1990

Kessler, Leo, *The Iron Fist*, Futura, London, 1977

Kleine, Egon and Kuhn, Volkmar, *Tiger*, Motorbuch Verlag, Stuttgart, 1990

Lefdevre, Eric, *Panzers in Normandy: Then and Now*, After the Battle, London, 1984

Lehman, Rudolf and Tieman Ralf, *The Leibstandarte IV/1*, J.J. Fedorowicz, Manitoba, 1993

MacDonald, Charles B., *The Battle of the Bulge*, Weidenfeld & Nicolson, London, 1984

McKee, Alexander, *Caen: Anvil of Victory*, Souvenir Press, London, 1964

Marshall, S.L.A., *Bastogne: The First Eight Days*, Center of US Military Hisory, US Army, Washington DC, 1996

Mellenthin, F.W., *Panzer Battles*, Futura, London, 1977

Meyer, Hubert, *Hitlerjugend*, J.J. Fedorowicz, Manitoba, 1994

Mitchell, Samuel, *Hitler's Legions*, Leo Cooper, London, 1985

Lord Montgomery of El Alamein, *Normandy to the Baltic*, Hutchinson, London, 1947

Pallud, Jean Paul, *Battle of the Bulge: Then and Now*, After the Battle, London, 1983

Quarrie, Bruce, *The Ardennes Offensive: Northern Sector*, Osprey, Oxford, 1999

Reynolds, Michael, *Steel Inferno*, Spellmount, Staplehurst, 1997

Reynolds, Michael, *Men of Steel*, Spellmount, Staplehurst, 1999

Ripley, Tim, *Steel Storm*, Sutton Publishing, Stroud, 2000

Rissik, David, *The DLI at War*, The Durham Light Infantry, Durham, 1952

Ryan, Cornelius, *A Bridge Too Far*, Hamish Hamilton, 1974

Saunders, Tim, *Hill 112*, Leo Cooper, Barnsley, 2001

Sydnor, Charles, *Soldiers of Destruction: The SS Totenkopf Division 1933–45*, Princeton University Press, 1977

Trout, Ken, *Tank!*, Robert Hale, London, 1985

Wilmot, Chester, *Struggle for Europe*, Collins, London,1952

Zaloga, Steven, *Sherman*, Osprey, London, 1978

Zetterling, Niklas, *Normandy 1944*, J.J. Fedorowicz, Manitoba, 2000

Records of the Wehrmacht Inspector of Panzer Troops

War Diary of XXXXVIII Panzer Corps, December 1943

German Reports Series, 18 Volumes, US Army

*History of the Second World War*, Purnell & Sons, 1966–1974

# INDEX

## PICTURE CREDITS